WINNING
LACROSSE
FOR GIRLS

The Winning Sports for Girls Series

Winning Basketball for Girls, Fourth Edition

Winning Lacrosse for Girls, Second Edition

Winning Soccer for Girls, Third Edition

Winning Softball for Girls, Second Edition

Winning Track and Field for Girls, Second Edition

Winning Volleyball for Girls, Third Edition

WINNING
LACROSSE
FOR GIRLS

SECOND EDITION

Becky Swissler

Foreword by
Katie Bergstrom

Head Coach, Lacrosse and Field Hockey,
Director of Girls' Athletics,
Germantown Friends School
Philadelphia, Pennsylvania

A MOUNTAIN LION BOOK

☑Checkmark Books®
An imprint of Infobase Publishing

WINNING LACROSSE FOR GIRLS, Second Edition

Checkmark Books
An imprint of Facts On File, Inc.
132 West 31st Street
New York NY 10001

Library of Congress Cataloging-in-Publication Data
Swissler, Becky.
    Winning lacrosse for girls / Becky Swissler ; foreword by Katie Bergstrom — 2nd ed.
      p. cm. — (The winning sports for girls series)
    Includes bibliographical references and index.
    ISBN-13: 978-0-8160-7712-0 (hardcover : alk. paper)
    ISBN-10: 0-8160-7712-6 (hardcover : alk. paper)
    ISBN-13: 978-0-8160-7713-7 (pbk. : alk. paper)
    ISBN-10: 0-8160-7713-4 (pbk. : alk. paper)
  1. Lacrosse for girls. I. Title.
   GV989.15.S95   2009
   796.347082—dc22   2008051346

Checkmark Books are available at special discounts when purchased in bulk quantities for businesses, associations, institutions, or sales promotions. Please call our Special Sales Department in New York at (212) 967-8800 or (800) 322-8755.

You can find Chelsea House on the World Wide Web at http://www.chelseahouse.com

Text design by Erika K. Arroyo
Cover design by Alicia Post
Photographs by Jesse Soifer
Illustrations by Sholto Ainslie

Printed in the United States of America

Bang Hermitage 10 9 8 7 6 5 4 3 2 1

This book is printed on acid-free paper.

All links and Web addresses were checked and verified to be correct at the time of publication. Because of the dynamic nature of the Web, some addresses and links may have changed since publication and may no longer be valid.

CONTENTS

ACKNOWLEDGMENTS

Special thanks to Germantown Friends School director of girls' athletics and head lacrosse coach Katie Bergstrom, the *Winning Lacrosse for Girls* consulting coach, for contributing her time and energy to this project. Thanks also to Liz Waldron, assistant coach, and Katie for coordinating the photography session that featured four of her varsity lacrosse players (see below, clockwise from left): Sadye Stern, Betsy Sachs, Lucie Rabinowitz, and Samie Francis. Special thanks to photographer Jesse Soifer.

FOREWORD

What is the nature of this game of lacrosse that has held my attention and prompted my devotion ever since I picked up a stick nearly two decades ago? How would I describe its unique appeal and my undiminished passion for the game? Is it my innate love of competition? Or is it the physical and mental challenge that gets me firing on all cylinders?

For one, I know that lacrosse is the ultimate team game. Every player is important regardless of her position on the field. It's true that everyone notices the player who attacks the goal and fires off a shot, but smart players and astute fans alike know the value of the attacker's hustling teammate who backs up the shot on goal and runs down the ball. Her hustle and heads-up play returns possession of the ball to the offense, which is so integral to the team's success. Such a play is comparable to that of basketball player who pulls down a rebound so her team's offensive can reset and run its plays. Much of the game's actions are akin to the athleticism found in other sports.

The thrill of leaping in the air to snatch a ball while being closely guarded is much like a volleyball player rising above the net to spike a ball that puts away a point. Players who have quick feet and agility stop the fastest of attackers on the crease much the way a third baseman in softball steps quickly left and right to cut off her opponent's bid for a base hit. The unique appeal of lacrosse springs from the fact that it is a sport in which a speedster or leaper or hustler—in fact, almost any type of athlete—can find a position to play. It is fluid and fast paced when it comes to its mosaic of actions and plays but democratic and inclusive when it comes to those who take up the positions to play the game. It beckons to aspiring athletes who are at times unsure of their special talents and abilities: "You bring the heart and desire. We'll find just the spot for you."

I am certain that lacrosse is the ultimate game for the multitasker, the player who can run the field all the while looking for and anticipating the exact moment to make that split-second pass to a cutting teammate. Lacrosse welcomes and rewards the athlete whose superior eye-hand coordination allows her to literally vacuum up bouncing, rolling loose balls. And lacrosse celebrates the athlete who has what I term "pure grit," which is determination and a can-do attitude that brings more balls into her stick all the while fending off fierce opponents whose flailing sticks are competing for possession.

As a player I loved the fast pace of lacrosse. One of my intangible skills was anticipating plays; I had what coaches call a feel for the game. It was so much fun competing for the ball. I got it, I lost it, I got it again. What a blast! My mother and aunts played lacrosse in their youth. When they told stories about their playing days they were always smiling and laughing. I just knew it was a game that I wanted to play.

I grew up competing in lacrosse, basketball, and field hockey. When I played lacrosse in middle school and high school I *first* mastered the art of playing defense. I discovered that communicating and working closely with my fellow defenders were immensely rewarding. I also found great satisfaction in practicing by myself. I would spend hours and hours in my backyard at night under floodlights practicing stick work and shooting on goal.

In college as a member of the women's lacrosse team at Columbia University my coach took notice of my accurate passing and shooting and asked me to play attack. I never looked back. I had the privilege of leading Columbia's hockey and lacrosse teams in most goals scored, but the greater privilege was working with such amazing athletes who made me a better player. The friendships that were developed on the field meant more than any record. And the mutual love of the sport shared with my teammates so many years ago remains today a powerful, binding force. This is a phenomenon that you cannot duplicate in any other environment.

I was one of the pioneer athletes at Columbia University, playing on the first Division I teams that the school fielded in lacrosse and field hockey. We played our hearts out and enjoyed every minute but our early seasons were mostly about building character. Our coach's words inspired us to our first victory: "Win today, walk together forever." Her words rang true. Our first team victory and our memories of it cannot be taken away by anyone. My most memorable moment was in our first season I scored a goal in the waning seconds of a game against a national powerhouse Princeton University team. The goal, which avoided a shutout, resulted from the all-out hustle of one of our defenders who fed me the ball. It was a little victory and a powerful reminder to never give up and to keep playing till the final whistle blows.

Now as the athletic director and head lacrosse coach at Germantown Friends School in Philadelphia, Pennsylvania, I have the honor and pleasure of passing along what I learned from the many awesome coaches who taught me. But just as important I try to instill in my players that learning begins with keeping an open and inquisitive mind.

Our lacrosse program is about building character and learning, but we also know how to win. Our lacrosse team has won 16 league championships, including two in the past three years. Our girls know the value of training hard and developing proper technique. They often devise their own exercises and drills that not only raise their fitness levels and playing skills but also bring members of the team closer.

Our players understand that their success on the field begins with preparation. They work diligently, practicing individual skills and team plays, and they expect good results when they take the field for games. Each time that our players step on the field they expect more of themselves than the time before. This drive to improve, to excel, to achieve in each player her personal best is an incredible mind-set for young women to take forward in their lives.

For those who aspire to be an accomplished player, *Winning Lacrosse for Girls* is a good way to learn the basic skills that are necessary. The book also presents tactics and strategies for the offense and defense. Players of all levels—from beginners to advanced—will find valuable instruction and insightful tips that can serve as the tools for getting to the next level. A reader can study this information, apply it diligently on the practice field and in games, and make herself the best player she can be. Easy-to-follow photographs demonstrating the skills and drills accompany much of the instructions.

There is more to this book than providing players with the tools to reach their ultimate talent level. *Winning Lacrosse for Girls* is also for parents who want to read and learn about the sport. Lacrosse is growing across the United States, especially in middle schools and high schools where new players and coaches are taking up the sport. *Winning Lacrosse for Girls* is the perfect companion for these new players and coaches. It is not only a first stop for new coaches but also a handy refresher for experienced ones. Among the many drill, tactics, and techniques on the following pages there is likely a new one that is worth putting into one's playbook.

You wouldn't be holding this book in your hand if you didn't have an interest in lacrosse and a curiosity about how to play the game. So turn the page and get started. The game will enthrall you, challenge you, and, most of all, reward you in more ways than you can imagine.

Katie Bergstrom
Head Coach, Lacrosse and Field Hockey
Director of Girls' Athletics
Germantown Friends School
Philadelphia, Pennsylvania

INTRODUCTION

When I began playing lacrosse, I trotted out to the field with my wooden stick, strings pulled tight in the pocket. The top of the ball, when tucked into the stick head, had to be at least two inches above the sidebars of the pocket. So in order to move around the field and maintain possession, you had to cradle the ball completely across your body, swinging both arms and the stick alternately out to either side as you ran. Only by moving the stick in a complete semicircle in front of your body could you create enough momentum to keep the ball inside the tight pocket.

Today, sticks are no longer made of wood. They are made of plastic, titanium, or aluminum. The pocket is designed to sag, so the ball can settle in while the player runs around the field—no full-swing cradling needed. The ability to travel with the ball set in the crosse liberates a player's movements as she cruises down the field, allowing her to try new moves and be creative.

Set amidst this fast-moving evolution of lacrosse's technique and equipment is one constant: the game's free-flowing nature. Yes, the game is changing, but the spirit remains the same. The guardians of the game are reviewing, reconsidering, and revising the rules in an effort to ensure the fluidity and freedom of the game. What an amazing time to be playing this sport!

Winning Lacrosse for Girls is the perfect resource for a beginner who wants to join in the fun of this unique sport, as well as for players who are looking to step it up a notch. Starting with the basics, you will learn how to pick up the stick, how to cradle and how to dodge. Other chapters are devoted to passing and receiving, checking the ball carrier, team offense, team defense, shooting, and goalkeeping. There is also a section on the history and rules of the game, as well as a conditioning chapter dedicated to getting you in the best physical shape possible to play the sport. Each chapter takes an in-depth look at the specific area, providing step-by-step instruction for getting started and advice from successful college coaches. There are numerous drills, techniques, and tips for playing well—and playing smart.

And even if you've been playing the sport for a few years, *Winning Lacrosse for Girls* demonstrates and explains advanced instruction, including advanced shots and more sophisticated offensive and defensive styles. All will help you progress and excel on the field. Remember, there's always a next level to strive for in this game, and this book offers great advice on how to get there.

In preparing the material for this book I spent many hours interviewing coaches and players, and basically connecting with everyone and anyone who has ever played lacrosse. No matter the age or playing level, they all share an overwhelming enthusiasm for the sport—a passion that surfaces time and again. When they talk about lacrosse, they stress the free-flowing movement of the game, the enjoyment of the sport, the importance of having fun, the value of creativity in play, and the exhilaration of just being a part of it all.

It's a testament to lacrosse that practically everyone who has picked up a stick has continued to be thoroughly taken with the game and has such wonderful things to say about it. In the presence of these coaches and players who are overrun with passion and sincerity for the beauty of the game, I can only conclude that lacrosse is helping to create not just amazing athletes, but amazing people, as well.

One of my goals in writing *Winning Lacrosse for Girls* is that the book will help instill enthusiasm, passion, and knowledge of lacrosse in the hearts' of beginners, and that the tradition of this beautiful game will continue to grow.

1

History and Rules

A BRIEF HISTORY

Lacrosse is the oldest organized sport in North America. It originated with the Native Americans during the 1400s. Tribes in different regions of North America played different versions of lacrosse, or *baggataway,* as they called it. Native Americans in the southeast—the Cherokee, Choctaw, Chickasaw, Creek, and Seminole, to name a few—played with two sticks, one in each hand. The ball was a soft, round mass of deerskin, and players held the ball between the two sticks made of wood or leather.

Tribes living around the Great Lakes—the Ojibwe, Menominee, Potawatomi, Sauk, and Fox, for example—played with one three-foot long stick that had a round, closed pocket, about three to four inches in diameter. The ball was carved from wood, burnt and then scraped into shape.

The southeastern and Great Lakes tribes often played in flat grassy fields with no boundaries. Goals were sometimes farther than one mile away from each other. There was no limit to the amount of people on a team, as long as there were equal numbers of players on both sides, so teams numbered from a few warriors to hundreds or thousands. Because there were so many people on the field, some players often didn't come near—or even see—the ball. The objective for these "off-ball" players was to injure the opponent with their sticks. This kept them in shape and focused their wartime skills. Occasionally, women played, usually apart from men.

The third form of "lacrosse" originated among the Iroquois and New England tribes. The Iroquois, located in the area known today as upstate New York and southern Ontario, were originally made up of six nations called the Iroquois Confederacy. Players held one stick at least three feet long with a triangular split at the top, which was netted to form a pocket. The Iroquois Confederacy teams appeared to be more organized than the other tribes. They established a set limit of 12 to 15 players per team, and created goals roughly 120 yards apart. Sometimes, they used a pole, tree, or rock for a goal. Other times, they had two goalposts, about six to nine feet apart. Clearly, the Iroquois style of play is the original precursor to modern-day lacrosse.

However in all tribes, there was no official with a stop clock to time the competitions—games sometimes lasted up to three days!

More Than a Sport, a Tradition

Regardless of the tribe or region of play, lacrosse was more than a sport; it was an important tradition to all Native Americans. There were countless reasons why tribes played the game.

Lacrosse was considered a physical, emotional, and spiritual training ground for all aspects of life. Native tribes often asked animal spirits to help them during the game. A player might wear a hawk feather to aid him in his swiftness, or a bear claw to make him strong. In some regions women played alongside the men; in other areas women had separate games; and still in other regions only men played while wives, daughters, mothers, and sisters watched the competitions.

Native Americans played lacrosse for medicinal reasons, believing that the strength, endurance, and agility involved in the sport promoted a healthy body, mind, and spirit. The same theory applied on a broader level too; a tribe playing the ball game together was a healthy one. They learned to work together to achieve success. If the Natives fell upon a particularly rough time, they would turn to the spiritual game to chase away disease, or to raise the spirits of the tribe. They also believed that the grace and beauty of the game provided an outlet with which they could communicate with the spiritual world.

Native Americans also played lacrosse as a way to stay in shape for hunting and war. In fact, the prewar and pre-*baggataway* rituals were very similar, if not identical, in some tribes.

All Native Americans turned to *baggataway* to resolve conflicts among families and tribes. Political disputes were often settled by a game of ball, with the winning team having the final say. Although this approach was intended to be a peaceful means of settling disagreements, there were instances when games resulted in war, and even death. In 1790, the Choctaw played the Creek, two southeastern tribes, in a match to settle a territory dispute regarding a beaver pond. After the Creeks were declared winners of the game, a battle broke out between the two tribes.

What's in a Name?

Jean de Brébeuf, a French Jesuit missionary, made the first non-Native documentation of the game in 1636. He saw the Huron tribe play lacrosse in what is now southeast Ontario. Almost 50 Native American tribes played the game throughout the region. By the early 1800s, French settlers named the game *la crosse* because the stick reminded them of a bishop's crozier (a bishop's staff), used in religious ceremonies. Shortly thereafter, lacrosse began to flourish. In 1834, the Caughnawaga tribe demonstrated the game in Montreal, and a local newspaper reported the new sport.

In 1844, Montreal's Olympic Club selected a men's lacrosse team to play against a Native American team. In 1856, the Montreal Lacrosse Club was founded. William George Beers, a Montreal dentist who was immediately taken with the sport, wrote the first set of official lacrosse rules in 1867. His rules called for 12 players per team, and replaced the Native ball with a hard, rubber ball. He also established a playing field with lined boundaries. Because of his determination and dedication to the sport, Beers is now referred to as the "father of lacrosse." Soon, techniques developed for such basic skills as passing, catching, and shooting. In addition, offensive team strategies emerged.

In 1867, due in large part to Beers's persistence in promoting the sport, the Canadian government made lacrosse the official sport of the country. Canada's National Lacrosse Association was founded, creating a national governing body for the sport. Within a year, the number of teams soared from six to 80. Soon the sport spread to the United States, Europe, Australia, and New Zealand, and by 1892, the English Lacrosse Union was formed. In the 1930s, Canadians began playing lacrosse indoors, and it remains a popular variation today.

Girls Join in the Fun

Women's lacrosse originated in the United Kingdom, where female physical educators recognized the value of the sport. Frances Jane Dove, Head Mistress of St. Leonard's School for Girls in St. Andrew's, Scotland, was the first instructor to include lacrosse in a secondary school curriculum. In 1890, St. Leonard's had its own girl's team. The first women's lacrosse game was played on English soil. Many of the rules that the men played by were changed. There was no body checking and no lined boundaries, which created more room to run, dodge, and cradle the ball. The form of play was free flowing and graceful. In this sense, women's lacrosse most closely resembles the early game played by the Native Americans.

Soon other high schools adopted the sport for their young women. By 1912, the Ladies Lacrosse Association was established. Women's lacrosse was on its way—at least in England!

Taking It Overseas

English women weren't pushing for the sport to take off in their homeland only, but in the United States as well. Many English women traveled to the United States to spread knowledge of the sport. In addition, many young women from America studied in England, and upon their return home, spread the news of women's lacrosse. Americans were slow to accept it. People immediately compared it to men's lacrosse, without so much as having seen the female version of the game. In many people's minds, the sport was too rough and masculine for women to play.

Although women's lacrosse was not easily accepted in mainstream United States, women's field hockey was. Many of the early proponents of women's lacrosse were also field hockey stars, so they used their leverage in the sporting community to promote lacrosse as a woman's sport. These advocates pointed out the differences between men and women's lacrosse, emphasizing that there was no body contact or checking in the women's game, and that players depended on superior stick skill and swiftness as opposed to brute strength. It was considered a graceful undertaking. Because the girls were running in an upright position, it was also promoting good posture, as well as the unselfish attitude fostered by team sports.

Because of the differences between the men's and women's games, female field players were not required to wear the same bulky protective gear that is necessary for men to wear. Women often played in skirts, which only supported the idea that it was, in fact, a sport fit for ladies.

Leaders in the Field

It would be impossible to credit the growth of women's lacrosse to just one of the pioneers of the sport. It took many efforts and many different people to nurture the sport in the United States.

Constance M. K. Applebee is attributed with introducing field hockey to young women all over the world. She ran a camp in the Pocono Mountains to teach young girls the sport, and in 1925, she invited Joyce Cran Barry to come over from England to be an instructor at the camp. Barry was not only a field hockey standout, but a lacrosse star as well. She began introducing lacrosse to the young woman at the Pocono camp, and other field hockey camps around the northeast region. On the day she was to return to England after the camp was over, she was offered (and accepted) a job coaching field hockey at Wellesley College. She used her position at Wellesley to further promote lacrosse, and soon there was a women's lacrosse team at Wellesley.

But Bryn Mawr College (outside Philadelphia) is home of the first collegiate women's lacrosse team in the United States. In 1926, Rosabelle Sinclair, a graduate of St. Leonard's School for Girls, introduced women's lacrosse to Bryn Mawr. By 1928, Sinclair had spread knowledge of the sport to other high schools and colleges in the Philadelphia and Baltimore area. She was instrumental in the development of women's club lacrosse teams.

In the summer of 1931, the United States Women's Lacrosse Association (USWLA) was founded at Applebee's camp in the Poconos, and Barry was the organization's first president. Women's lacrosse now had a legitimate regulating body: one organization to create a set list of rules for the sport. The USWLA governed collegiate and club level play. In 1933, the USWLA held its first national tournament in Greenwich, Connecticut.

In the mid-1930s, men and women's lacrosse began to differ greatly. The women's version remained true to the sport's origin, with an emphasis on passing and a prohibition on bodily contact. By contrast, men's rules began to allow body checking. As a result, men began to wear pads and other protective equipment, whereas women did not. In the decades since, men and women's lacrosse have continued to evolve as two distinctly different versions, each with its own appeal.

A Slow Growth

Following World War II, the United States had adult women association teams in New York, Philadelphia, Boston, Baltimore and West Chester. After World War II, Margaret Boyd, originally from England, devoted herself to teaching American women the sport. She traveled along the East Coast of the United States, offering clinics to women as she went. In 1972, she founded the International Federation of Women's Lacrosse Association (IFWLA), and was the organization's first president. The first Women's World Championship was held in 1969, which in 1982 became the Women's World Cup tournament.

SEE IT SPREAD

Women's lacrosse took off at the secondary school level in the middle of the 20th century. In 1940, 20 secondary schools supported a female lacrosse team. That number grew to 33 in 1949, 104 in 1957, and 240 in 1978. In 2000, more than 15,000 women were playing the sport at 600 high schools across the country.

By 2007, the numbers had skyrocketed. More than 81,000 women were playing lacrosse at 1,800 high schools, according to U.S. Lacrosse and the National Federation of State High School Associations. In the past decade, lacrosse has been the fastest-growing high school sport, the federation says. There are now more than 300 college lacrosse programs for women, triple the number two decades ago.

NCAA Records

In 1982, the National Collegiate Athletics Association (NCAA) took over the USWLA. Trenton State and the University of Massachusetts faced each other in the first NCAA women's lacrosse tournament. The game was played at Trenton State College in Ewing, New Jersey. The University of Massachusetts won 9-6. The 1982 tournament was for all schools with women's lacrosse. Since then, the NCAA has divided the level of play into three divisions: Division I, Division II, and Division III. Division I is the most competitive division.

Since the first NCAA tournament in 1982, the University of Maryland has won nine Division I Championships, appearing in 14 tournaments. The Division III tournament was established in 1985. Trenton State College (renamed the College of New Jersey in 1996) appeared in 15 of the 18 tournaments, winning 11 championships.

It wasn't until 2001 that the NCAA held a Division II tournament for women's lacrosse. West Chester appeared in both the 2001 and 2002 tournaments, winning the title in 2002.

RULES

Lacrosse is one of the most free-flowing games played on a field. There are, however, set rules by which all players must abide. The rules in this chapter are the women's official rules as detailed by U.S. Lacrosse, the national governing body of men's and women's lacrosse since 1998. Following these rules are the modified rules for youth girl's lacrosse. These rules are designed for beginners under the eighth grade level of play.

THE FIELD

The boundaries on a women's lacrosse field follow the natural boundaries of the land. The advised field size is 70 yards wide by 120 yards long. However, younger, less experienced girls may play on fields measuring 50 yards wide and 110 yards long. The official clearly determines the boundaries before the start of the game. Although most fields follow natural

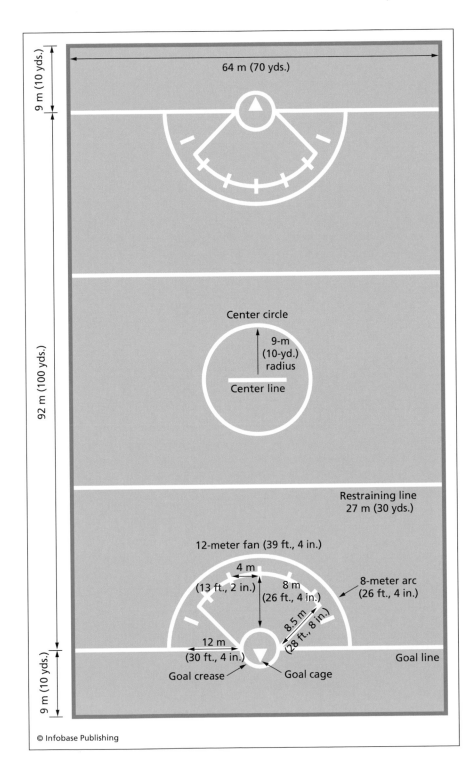

9 m (10 yds.)

64 m (70 yds.)

92 m (100 yds.)

Center circle

9-m
(10-yd.)
radius

Center line

Restraining line
27 m (30 yds.)

12-meter fan (39 ft., 4 in.)

4 m
(13 ft., 2 in.)

8 m
(26 ft., 4 in.)

8-meter arc
(26 ft., 4 in.)

8.5 m
(28 ft., 8 in.)

12 m
(30 ft., 4 in.)

Goal line

Goal crease

Goal cage

9 m (10 yds.)

boundaries such as tree lines, hills, or sidewalks, some fields with no such natural boundaries have painted sidelines and end lines. Anything beyond these lines, or the set natural boundaries determined by the teams and the ref, are out of bounds. The center circle is in the center of the field. This circle is equidistant from both the sides of the field and the two goals. The center circle is 10 yards in diameter.

Goals

The goals are set up 100 yards apart from each other. Unlike any other game, the field extends behind the goals an additional 10 yards. The goal line is a point of reference, not a boundary that cannot be crossed. The goal is positioned at the center of the goal line facing the center circle. The goal line continues out to either side of the net for 39 feet and 4 inches, and runs parallel to the end line and centerline of the field. A goal is scored when the ball passes over the plane of the goal line where the net is. If an offensive player shoots the ball and it bounces off the body of a defender, the goal is good. If, however, the ball deflects off the body of her offensive teammate, the goal does not count.

Goals are constructed of metal and are six feet high, six feet wide, and six feet deep. The back point or sides of the goal are pinned to the ground, and the structure is covered in netting around the back frame. In some cases, the goal has a flat iron base shaped in a V. These types of goals do not need to be pinned down. Although the field extends behind the goal, players can only score from the front of the goal that faces the center of the field.

There is a circle around each goal. This circle is called the goal circle, or crease. This is where the goalie stands to play the ball and defend the net.

Eight-Meter Arc

The eight-meter arc is the critical scoring area in front of the cage. The endpoints of the arc are where the crease meets the goal line to either side of the net. From these two points, the lines angle out and away from the goal for eight meters. An arc line on the field connects the endpoints of these two lines, forming an eight-meter arc in front of the cage. Defenders in the eight-meter arc must be within one stick length from their opponent, otherwise, after three seconds, the ref will call a three-second violation, which is a major foul.

Twelve-Meter Fan

The 12-meter fan is also a high scoring area. The 12-meter fan is a semicircle with its endpoints 12 meters to either side of the goal along the goal line.

An arc is painted on the field between these two endpoints, forming a semicircle in front of the goal. Officials use the 12-meter fan to position players after fouls are called. The eight-meter arc is within the 12-meter fan.

Restraining Line

There is a restraining line 30 yards in front of each goal. No more than seven offensive players and eight defensive players (including the goalie) can be within it at one time. This is an important rule to remember when recovering back on defense, or when an offensive attack is under way.

Team Areas

The team benches are stationed along the sideline off the field and on either side of the 50-yard line, also known as the centerline. Between the team benches is the official's table, which monitors all substitutions, goals, and penalties. Official time for the game is kept here.

POSITIONS

There are 12 players per team on the field during a women's lacrosse game. Unlike field hockey or soccer, the players do not start out on the same side of the field as their teammates, but rather are stationed around the field from one goal to the other, similar to the start of a basketball game. Players start the game matched up next to a player from the opposing team. The 12 positions, from offense to defense, are: first home, second home, third home, left attack wing, right attack wing, center, left defense wing, right defense wing, third man, coverpoint, point, and goalkeeper.

First Home

First home is the most offensive position on the field. Her first priority is to score. She starts the game closest to the offensive goal. First home has superior stick work because she is often in high-traffic and high-pressure situations. First home sets up plays behind the goal cage, waiting for her teammates to cut in front of the cage. When that happens, she passes the ball to them to create a scoring opportunity. She must protect the ball and keep it close to the goal to maintain pressure on the goalie. First home must be able to cut quickly in a limited space, always looking to shoot or find a teammate who can shoot. She needs to master all types of passes to avoid defenders.

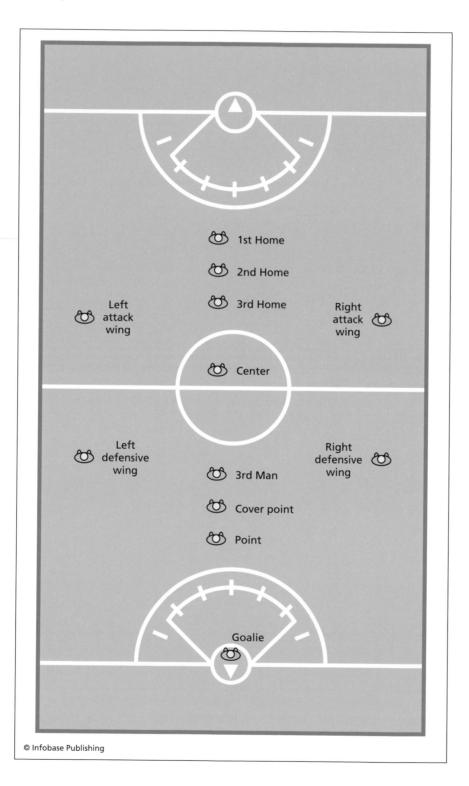

1st Home

2nd Home

3rd Home

Left attack wing

Right attack wing

Center

Left defensive wing

Right defensive wing

3rd Man

Cover point

Point

Goalie

Second Home

The second home makes things happen. Statistically, she has a lot of assists. (An assist is the last offensive pass before a goal is scored.) The second home shoots well from any angle and from any distance to goal. She is dependable and strong and also has excellent stick work. Second home also works from behind the goal cage. She must have excellent footwork, always staying in motion to receive or make a pass. Above all, she must be an outstanding ball handler, avoiding turnovers that waste scoring opportunities.

Third Home

Third home helps to transition the ball from defense to offense, and supports her offensive homes. She often assists in the goal scoring and sometimes shoots through to score herself. She needs to be a trusted leader who can initiate and maintain offensive pressure with her movement and passing.

Left and Right Attack Wings

Wings also transition the ball from the backfield to the offensive end. Wings do a lot of running, as they are depended upon by both offensive and defensive teammates. They must support both ends of the field and keep the two ends of the field connected. They need to stay alert. Often, wings receive the ball after a center draw, so they need to immediately move the ball downfield and look for scoring chances. Wings are usually the fastest players on the team because they constantly transition between the offensive and defensive ends of the field.

Left and Right Defense Wings

Defensive wings mark the opposing attack wings and keep them out of play from the ball. A good defender can mark her opponent out of the game, forbidding her teammates from passing the ball to her. Because she is marking an attack wing, a defensive wing also does a lot of running. Defensive wings have speed, endurance, and an intimidating attitude! A defensive wing must be extremely fast to keep up with charging offensive players. She needs to anticipate players' movements and quickly react. She looks for chances to start offensive fast breaks and can cross midfield to help with the charge.

Center

The center is the strongest player on the field. She starts the game with the draw, and controls the middle of the field. She plays both offense and defense, and is always on the move. Center is integral in transitioning the ball down the field. This is another position that requires speed, endurance, and authority. Often, she is the team's most complete player. Because she's stationed at the center of the field, she must be equally adept on offense and defense. She needs good vision of the entire field to sense and react to the unfolding action.

Third Man

The main responsibility of the third man is to mark the opposing team's third home. She must be quick to intercept passes and have excellent footwork and speed to stay with her mark. A third man has great reflexes, and often jumps in front of her mark to reach for an interception. Her main responsibility is to disrupt the offensive flow and look for chances to get her team back on offense. She can cross midfield to help with an offensive charge.

Coverpoint

The coverpoint marks the opposing team's second home player. The coverpoint is excellent at marking and has great footwork. She also works with the goalie and receives clears from the goalie. She plays smart defense and moves the ball away from the goal to the offense for a transition play. She needs excellent one-on-one coverage skills to keep defenders from advancing near the goal. When she receives a pass from her goalie, she must quickly look up field for teammates to receive a pass and start an offensive break.

Point

Point is the most defensive field player on the team. She marks the opposing team's first home. She is great at marking and checking. She also works hand in hand with the goalie and must be a good communicator. Aside from the goalie, she is the most defensive player on the field and has a good view of what is happening. Her viewpoint is valuable, so listen to her advice! She's the last line of defense before the goalie. She must be tenacious in marking opponents, stick checking, and blocking shots. The point must always stay alert because one slipup can lead to a goal for the opposing team. She rarely strays far from the goal area.

Goalie

First and foremost, goalies protect the goal and lead the defensive communication. A goalie is always telling her defenders who to mark and letting them know when someone is open, or when someone should slide

over and double team an offensive player. Within the goal circle, or crease, the goalie uses any part of her body to stop the ball from entering the net. Goalies also must be aggressive and at times come out of the crease to go after a wide shot or possibly to intercept the ball. Goalies have good stick work, quick reflexes, and a no-fear attitude.

EQUIPMENT

All players wear rubber soled shoes or cleats; no metal spikes are allowed. All players (including the goalie) must wear a mouthguard. Field players have the option of wearing close fitting gloves, nose guards, soft headgear and protective eye goggles. The goalie must always wear a helmet, mouthguard, facemask, throat protector, and chest protector. Goalies are also allowed to wear additional protective pads on their arms, legs, shoulders, hands, and chest.

The Stick and Ball

For many years, the lacrosse stick, also called the crosse, was made of wood. The sticks were heavy and didn't allow for quick passes. Now, virtually all sticks are made of plastic, titanium, or aluminum. They are much lighter and have helped the game become faster and more exciting. Sticks are 35½ inches to 43¼ inches long. Defenders often prefer longer sticks, while offensive players like shorter ones. The top of the stick, the head, is molded for greater control of the ball. The head cannot have a deep pocket. When the ball is resting in the pocket and the stick is parallel to the ground, the top of the ball must be visible. The goalie's stick is 35½ inches to 48 inches long.

RULES OF THE GAME

Time

In high school, lacrosse games are 50 minutes long, with two 25-minute halves and one timeout per half. At the college level, the game extends to 60 minutes with two 30-minute halves. The clock stops after every goal and after every whistle in the last two minutes of the half. If a team is leading by 10 goals or more, then there is no clock stoppage, except during the last two minutes of play.

Officials

Ideally, three officials regulate the game: one field umpire, one scorer, and one timer. The field umpire moves with the play on the field and calls fouls and out of bounds. The scorer is positioned near each goal and determines when goals are scored, or when there is a foul in the critical scoring area. The timer keeps a record of when the game starts, how many timeouts are used and when the game finishes. Occasionally, only a field umpire and scorer officiate the game.

Boundaries

Although women's lacrosse follows the natural boundaries of the land, the field is usually marked with visual guides to aid the referee in determining where those boundaries are. These guides can either be painted lines or flags pinned in the ground. As mentioned before, the field must be at least 70 yards wide by 120 yards long.

The Draw

A lacrosse game starts at the center of the field with a draw. The two opposing centers on each team face each other in the middle of the center circle. The centers hold their sticks at waist level and parallel to the ground, with the backside of the stick pockets up against each other and touching. The centers stand with their dominant toe to the centerline, but not on it. The referee places the ball between the two pockets. Both players must remain motionless until they hear the referee's whistle. The ref steps back and blows the whistle, and the two centers force the ball up and away, each hoping to control the ball with her crosse and shovel pass it overhead to a teammate. For the draw to be legal, the ball must be hit higher than the players' heads. The centers are the only players allowed within the center circle during the draw. The draw also starts the second half of play and is used after every goal is scored. During the draw, only five players from each team, including the center, are permitted within the restraining lines.

Penalties

Once the ball is in play, teams attempt to advance toward the goals. The referees blow the whistle when the ball goes out of play, when a player commits a foul, or when a goal is scored. Whenever the whistle is blown, except for after a goal, every player on the field must freeze where they are.

Out of Bounds

If the ball is out of bounds, the player closest to the ball gets possession. If a player has intentionally thrown the ball out of bounds, the other team gets possession. If two opposing players are equidistant to the ball when it goes out of bounds, play is restarted with a throw. During the throw, the two closest players to the ball stand one meter apart from each other. The ref stands four to eight meters away and throws the ball up into the air. Whoever gets the ball first gains possession. All other players on the field must be at least four meters away from the two players involved in the throw.

A throw is also taken if a ball gets lodged in a player's clothes or if two players foul at the same time.

Safety First: No Body Contact

Offensively, players run, pass, and catch the ball to move it down the field toward their goal. Defensively, players check, mark, and intercept the ball to stop the offense from advancing. A check is a controlled action that a defender uses to knock the ball loose from her opponent's stick. The contact is stick to stick and is not intended to be dangerous in any way.

Stick checking requires skill and control. It takes a great deal of practice to perfect. The defender must hit the outside corner of the opposing player's stick pocket with her stick. The contact is intended to turn the offensive player's stick so the ball falls out. Stick checks should be short, quick jabs—no long backswing or sweeping follow-through. The defender must maintain her balance during the stick check, or she can fall and injure herself or the other player. A defender must be one step ahead of her opponent to execute a check. A defender can check from behind if the stick head—and movement of the check—is down and away from the attack player's head. She cannot reach across her opponent's body to check. Body checking and rough checking is strictly prohibited. Every player has a seven-inch sphere around her head—an invisible bubble that the opponent's stick cannot move into. During the check, a defender's stick must move away from that seven-inch bubble and the offender's face. The offender may not cradle the ball so close to her face so that it is impossible for the defender to safely execute a check.

Goalie

The goalkeeper is the only player who can play the ball with her hands, and she can only use her hands when she is within the goal crease. During play, the goalie might leave the crease to play the ball. If she does, she loses all her privileges and can only play the ball with her crosse, as the other field players do. A goalie shouldn't be afraid to leave the crease to intercept a pass or run down a ground ball. However, she should do so wisely. If a goalie leaves the crease and doesn't come up with the ball, the opposition has an open shot on goal. Once she decides to leave the crease, she can't hesitate in going after the ball. If the goalie is out of the goal circle, one other defender may enter the circle to defend the goal. This player is the deputy, and she is the only person other than the goalie allowed in the crease (and only when the goalie has left the crease).

Substitution

Substitution may occur at any time during the game. This type of substitution is called "sub-on-the-fly." Subs come in at the 50-yard line in the middle of the field. The official timetable keeps track of substitutions.

FOULS

Fouls are classified as either major or minor. When a player commits a major or minor foul, the ref blows her whistle and everyone freezes.

Free Position

When a player fouls her opponent within the eight-meter arc, the opponent is awarded a free position. The player who was fouled gets the ball, and the player who committed the foul is moved four meters behind her opponent. All other players are four meters away from the ball. The ref blows the whistle again, and the player with the ball may run, pass, or shoot as she chooses.

If a minor foul occurs in the critical shooting area, the player who was fouled takes an indirect free position, which means that she must first pass before a shot is taken.

Slow Whistle

If the defense commits a major foul in the critical scoring area, the ref throws her flag, but holds her whistle. This is called a slow whistle. Play continues, giving the offense an opportunity to score a goal. If the defense comes up with the ball, the ref blows her whistle and awards the offense a free position. If any foul occurs which threatens the safety of another player, the whistle is blown immediately. When a free position is awarded within the 12-meter fan, the ref clears a penalty lane between the player taking the free position and the goal.

When a goal circle foul occurs (see below), the player fouled takes an indirect free position 12 meters out to either side of the goal, in line with the goal line.

Minor Fouls

Goal circle fouls are minor fouls. A goal circle foul occurs when any part of an offensive or defensive player's body or stick crosses over the goal crease line and enters the goal circle. The goalie and the deputy are the only players allowed to cross this line. Other forms of goal circle fouls can occur: when the goalie keeps the ball in the circle for more than 10 seconds, the goalie reaches beyond the circle to play the ball, the goalie pulls the ball into the circle while she has any part of her body on the ground outside the circle, or when the goalie steps back into the circle with the ball after playing the ball outside the circle. Basically, the goalie can leave the circle to play the ball, but she cannot bring the ball back to her crease. If she chooses to leave the circle, she must do so entirely before playing the ball, she cannot have one foot in the crease and one foot out. A goalie with the ball outside of her crease can re-enter by dumping the ball into her crease first.

It is also a minor foul for a player to use her foot or crosse to guard a grounded ball. A player who takes one hand off the stick to hold an opponent away, referred to as warding, is also guilty of a minor foul. An empty crosse check (checking an opponent's stick when the ball is not in it) is also a minor foul.

Other minor fouls include touching the ball with the hand, throwing the stick, executing an illegal draw, playing without a stick, intentionally delaying the game, intentionally throwing the ball out of bounds, and playing without a mouthguard.

Major Fouls

Most major fouls are related to playing the game too roughly and causing bodily harm when checking. Any rough or careless checking is considered a major foul. Slashing (which occurs when the defender swings her stick with intent to harm) is a major foul. A player can be called for this regardless of whether or not her stick touches her opponent's stick or body. It is also a major foul to hold the stick across the face or neck of an opponent. Holding the stick of an opponent is also a major foul. Blocking and charging are major fouls. A player is guilty of blocking when she places herself in the path of an oncoming opponent without giving that opponent enough time to change her direction. Charging occurs when an offensive player charges or pushes into her opponent without attempting to change her path.

It is also a major foul for a defender to remain in the eight-meter arc for more than three seconds unless she is closely marking her opponent (she must be within one stick length of her opponent). If a defender is not closely marking her opponent and is in the path between the ball-carrying opponent and the goal, the ref will call obstruction of free space, which is another major foul.

Taking a dangerous shot is an offensive major foul. A shooter must be aware of where the goal is and must not aim for another field player or directly at the goalkeeper's head.

Warning Cards

There are three penalty cards in lacrosse which the ref distributes as needed. A yellow card is a warning for poor sportsmanship, rough play, or continued disruption of the game. If a player ignores the yellow card warning and continues to misbehave on the field, she will next receive a red card. A red card indicates suspension from the current game, and possibly from future games. If a team is delaying the game intentionally, the team captain receives a green card. The green card is directed toward the entire team.

MODIFIED RULES FOR GIRLS

US Lacrosse established a modified set of rules for girls' youth lacrosse in an effort to create a solid, safe environment in which to learn the sport. The modified checking rule for youth players states that there is no stick checking for players below the seventh grade level. Players at this level focus on the basics: proper body positioning, footwork, marking, cradling, catching, and throwing.

In the seventh- and eighth-grade level, players participate in a modified form of stick checking. The modified stick-checking rule dictates that players only stick check when the cradling stick is below shoulder level. In addition, the checking motion is down and away from the attack player's body. Any stick checking done above shoulder level in a motion toward the player with the ball is considered a foul. Umpires and coaches must enforce the modified rules.

US Lacrosse emphasizes that stick-to-stick contact does not necessarily mean that a player is illegally checking. In certain cases, an attack player may cradle into a defender's stick, causing the sticks to make contact. The sound of the sticks colliding may not indicate an illegal check, but rather good defensive positioning. Similarly, when an attack player is attempting to throw the ball, the defender may hold her stick up to intercept the ball. The follow through of the attack player's stick could hit the defender's stick. Again, this contact is not illegal. Only when the defender haphazardly swings her stick at the attack player in a manner that is dangerous and violates the modified rules should the referee interfere with play.

2
The Basics

LACROSSE IS OFTEN REFERRED TO AS "THE FASTEST GAME ON TWO FEET." This is a well-earned reputation. The basis of lacrosse is footwork. In this game you move constantly, transitioning from offense to defense. You always know where the ball is in relation to your offensive goal, and the location of your defensive mark. There is a lot happening on the lacrosse field, and it happens very quickly.

THE CROSSE

Before learning the fundamentals of offensive and defensive footwork and body positioning, it is necessary to first understand the relationship between the stick, or crosse, and your body.

Carrying Your Crosse

The top, netted pocket of your crosse (the head) is where you carry the ball. The opposite end of the stick is called the butt end. Most players use a plastic, aluminum, or titanium stick with a molded head above the netted pocket.

How you hold the stick is incredibly important. Denise Wescott, Head Coach at Delaware University, offers the following

Carrying your crosse

advice when gripping the crosse: "Players want their grip to be loose. Hold the stick like you're holding a bird; you want it to be tight enough so the bird won't fly away, but not so hard that you would kill the bird." Cradling is the most important skill in lacrosse. It's the act of quickly but smoothly rocking the top of the stick back and forth. This creates centrifugal force, which keeps the ball in the pocket as the player runs, passes, or shoots. Without mastering cradling, a player can't control the ball and can't be an effective player.

Players should hold the top of the stick a few inches below the pocket with their dominant hand. The other hand should be near the bottom of the stick for control. Players should relax their arms and wrists and gently twist the top of the stick back and forth, keeping it near the side of their head. Never let the stick get in front of your body because it's much harder to control the ball. We'll discuss cradling more in chapter 3.

Set Position

With that in mind, hold the stick vertically in front of you with the open pocket facing forward (away from you). Place your dominant hand, the hand you write or throw with, six inches below the pocket of the stick alongside the shaft. The back of your hand faces away from the stick toward the side. The top of your palm, where your fingers join the palm, lines up with the side of the shaft. Close your fingers around the stick, extending your index finger slightly up the crosse toward the pocket. Bring your thumb around the other side of the stick so your hand forms a loose fist with the crosse resting at the base of your fingers. Coach Wescott encourages beginners to remember to drop the top wrist and move the index finger up the shaft, which keeps the top elbow down and ensures that the stick sits in the bottom part of the fingers. Pull the stick head back and cock your wrist so the stick head is at an angle toward the sky and the butt end of the stick is on a diagonal toward the middle of your body, crossing in front of

Set, or triple threat, position

your hips. Drop your top hand shoulder down and back, and keep your elbow pointing down and slightly back. The stick head is off your body toward your dominant side, below the plane of your head with the pocket angled upward. Extend your non-dominant arm down on a diagonal toward your top hand side and close your hand loosely around the butt end of the stick. Lock your lower arm in this position near the hip. The backside of your lower hand is facing forward.

Keep your feet facing forward and lead with your lower arm shoulder. This means that your nondominant shoulder is forward. Twist your upper body toward the side your stick is on.

Always keep the stick on this diagonal line to the side of your body with the stick head behind your dominant side shoulder. The open pocket of the stick is facing forward. This is the set position, also referred to as the triple threat position because you can pass, cradle, or shoot from this position at a moment's notice. Always hold the stick off to the top hand side of your body. This positions your body to naturally protect your crosse and the ball from oncoming defense.

BODY POSITIONING

Body positioning is an incredibly important part of lacrosse. When you are out of position, an opponent is more likely to beat you. You are also more likely to foul your opponent. Nine times out of 10, a foul occurs because someone is out of position. To truly understand body positioning, forget about your stick for one second. Put your stick aside and concentrate only on what your body is doing and how.

Offensive Positioning

When playing lacrosse, you're always on the go. Offensive positioning in this sport is a reflection of this. Stand with your feet shoulder width apart and knees slightly bent. Bending your knees lowers your center of gravity, which creates a balanced, ready stance. Center your weight down the middle of your body and keep your weight on the balls of your feet. With bent knees and weight on the front of your feet, you are in position to charge in any direction and move at top speed. Keep your body loose to maintain flexibility in your stance.

Because this is a 100 percent running game, use a lead foot in your offensive stance. A lead foot means one foot is slightly ahead of the other so that you can easily take off into a sprint. The front foot is your lead foot. If you are unsure of which foot is your lead, stand up straight with your weight evenly distributed on both feet. Have someone push you from behind. The foot that you automatically step out with first is your lead foot.

Defensive Positioning

The key to a strong defensive stance is balance. Every defender must be well balanced in order to react to the movements of the offense. Balance is found in a low, even stance. Center your weight down the middle of your body and stand on the balls of your feet. Your feet are slightly wider than shoulder width apart, and your knees are bent so you are low to the ground. Anticipate where the ball is headed so you always have an idea of what is happening, even if the ball is not in your immediate area. As a defender, you must always be aware of where your mark is. Just like basketball, lacrosse is predominantly player-to-player sport, so you must pay attention to what your mark is doing.

FOOTWORK

Equally important to body positioning is footwork. Coach Wescott says, "Foot skills, agility, and speed are nine-tenths of the law in this game." Not only must your body be positioned correctly, but also your feet must be ready to go at all times. Foot skills require prac-tice, practice, and more practice. You can increase your speed, agility, and dexterity by practicing footwork techniques. "We've had kids that have been injured and haven't had a chance to do some of [the footwork skills] for awhile, and they say they can see a difference in their foot skills. They feel like they're moving better," says Coach Wescott.

One sure way to foul in lacrosse is to be lazy with your feet. Never sit back on your heels, but always stay positioned with your weight on the balls of your feet. Some footwork techniques are reserved for offensive or defensive situations, however one technique is used on either side of play: breaking down your steps.

Breaking Down Your Steps

Just like in basketball, field hockey, or soccer, you must be in control of your body as you approach the ball. If you are running at a full-on sprint, you have to break down your steps when you come near the ball. Otherwise, you won't have control of your actions, and will fly by the scene of play—or knock another player down! Whether offensively chasing a ball, or defensively chasing the player with the ball, you must begin to slow down when you come within five yards of your intended target.

Cut your stride in half and land your strides with your weight on the balls of your feet. Lift your knees high as you slow down. Your high knees act as a brake to your body. As you slow down and regain control of your movements, move your stick into position to play the ball.

OFFENSIVE FOOTWORK

There are five basic techniques in offensive footwork: changing pace, changing direction, stutter step, body fake, and a combination technique.

Changing Pace

This is a tried-and-true offensive footwork strategy. A simple way to throw off the defense is to change your running pace. If you are constantly changing your speed, a defender marking you becomes easily tired and confused. Begin running at half speed. Explode into a full sprint. Dig your toes into the ground and pump your arms hard to help in your take off to a sprint. Now shift down to a slow jog. Use the breakdown technique to slow your body down—land your stride on the balls of your feet and pull your knees up high. Hold your stick halfway down the shaft in your top hand as you sprint down the field. This one arm grip frees your arms to pump hard in the run and acceleration.

Practice changing the speed of your run so you can easily shift from one gear to the next. The quicker you transition, the better chance you have of getting away from your defender.

Changing Direction

A simple strategy for loosing defenders is to change your direction. It's a sure fire way to confuse the defender.

Begin by running straight down the field. To cut to the right, step down hard on your left foot and push off toward the right from the outside of your foot. Turn your hips and redirect your shoulders to the right as you push off. Extend your right foot out to the right and point your toes in the new direction. Step down on the ball of your right foot and explode to the right.

If you are changing your direction to move to the left, step down hard on your right foot, pushing off the outside of the foot. Turn your hips and redirect your shoulders to the left. Extend your left foot to the left with your toes pointing in the new direction. Step down on the ball of your left foot and explode in a sprint to the left.

Practice moving down the field in a Z, constantly cutting back and forth and working the balls of your feet and your ankles to quickly change direction.

Stutter Step

The stutter step is a momentary pause when your feet literally stutter—no ground is gained—in an effort to confuse your defender. This move is sometimes called a *deke* in ice hockey.

Stutter step with body fake *(above and following page)*

From a straight run, begin breaking down your steps as you approach the defender. You must be in control of your body to execute a stutter step, or deke. Step lightly on the ball of your right foot and pull your body so you aren't moving forward anymore. Bring your left foot up parallel to your right, if not slightly behind, so your feet are shoulder width apart. Step down lightly on the ball of your left foot. This is the stutter. Push off hard from the outside of your left foot to the right. Swivel your hips and extend your right foot out to the right, exploding into a sprint. Stride out on your right leg and land on the ball of your right foot. Continue sprinting ahead.

The stutter step is used in combination with a change of direction. Your momentary lag in speed and direction confuses the defender and forces her to stop moving and rethink what you are about to do.

Body Fake

An excellent way to fool the defense is to use a body fake. Your body language is always being evaluated and deciphered by the defense—they are watching your feet, arms, and head to determine what you are about to do. Control the movement of your feet and upper body and you will confuse this language and leave the defense in the dust. Body fakes consist of upper body pumps and hard foot fakes in the direction opposite to where you're heading.

If, for example, you are changing your direction to the right, you are going to step down hard on your left foot and push off to the right in the new direction. When you step down on the left foot, exaggerate that step so your lower body appears to be moving in that direction. Pump your head toward the left and look toward the left as if you truly are moving in that direction. Quickly pull back and move to the right. Your hard footwork, head pump, and eye contact to the left make the defender think you are definitely moving to the left, and she will shift over to cover that move. As she does this, you cut to the right. She is off balance, moving in the wrong direction, and has no chance of stopping you.

Throwing body fakes is an excellent way to fool opponents. Don't be afraid that you're over-exaggerating your moves. You can never fool a defender too much. On the other hand, if your fakes aren't obvious enough, the defender won't believe you—or worse yet, won't even notice!

Combinations

Use any mix of the above combinations to become a top-notch offensive star. "You need those foot skills for that quick first step when you're going on offense," says Coach Wescott. The basis of offensive success is footwork. Use it to your advantage. Prepare to change your direction, throw a body fake and shift to a top sprinting gear once you take off in the new direction.

DEFENSIVE FOOTWORK

Now that you're an unstoppable offender, become your own worst nightmare and work on your defensive footwork so that you will be able to stop any direction-changing, speed-altering, body-faking attack player that comes your way. Be aware of your opponent's efforts, and stay low and balanced in your stance so you can keep up with her. Your feet should be shoulder-width apart, knees bent, and weight balanced on the balls of your feet. Keep your arms to your sides with your elbows bent slightly. Now you're ready to move forward, backward, or side to side without losing your balance. Remember, defense is played with your feet, not your stick. Most defensive footwork skills focus on keeping the attack player in front of you, and changing your direction without losing your positioning. Says Coach Wescott, "You definitely need a quick change of direction defensively to be able to stay with a player." One of the most common defensive problems, according to Coach Wescott, are defensive players who stop moving their feet. Consider yourself a body in motion, and keep that body moving until the final whistle blows!

Drop Step

You always want to keep your attack mark in front of you. You also must give her a small cushion so that you can react to her movements. Just like in basketball, a drop step in lacrosse is a small diagonal step back and out to the side. This moves keeps your body in front of the attack player as she tries to move down the field.

Stand in the defensive stance with your stick up and out in front of you. Drop step first onto your right foot. Push off the outside of your left foot and step back and out to the right with your right foot. Swing your hips to the right so your upper body stays centered. Keep your knees bent as you swing your right foot back.

Now push off the outside of your right foot and swing your left foot back and out slightly to the left. Swing your hips to the left, always keeping your upper body centered to the attack player you are marking. Imagine a spot in the middle of your chest. Keep that spot so it is always facing your opponent. If your center is always facing her, you are centered.

If the attack player makes a move to go by you on your right, swing your hips open to the right and drop step back with your right foot. This diagonal step back keeps you in a good defensive position and keeps your opponent in front of you. Once you drop step, swivel your hips so your feet are moving in the same direction as your opponent. Keep your upper body facing your opponent.

Drop step

Slide Step

You must train your feet to take you exactly where you need to be in order to be in the best defensive stance. As described above, often times, an attack player changes her direction in an attempt to lose you. If she is moving across the field, use a slide step to laterally move with her.

In this move, your feet actually slide over the ground while your body remains in position to defend the attack player. Keep your upper body centered on your attack mark. Bend at your knees and at your waist so you are low and in a good defensive stance. Hold your stick out in front of you. Point your feet forward, facing the attack player.

To slide to the right, push off from the outside ball of your left foot. Step with bended knee laterally to the right with your right foot. Step down on the ball of your right foot and pull your left leg with bended knee in toward your body. Always keep your feet slightly wider than shoulder width apart. Continue this motion as you move with your opponent. To slide to the left, step off your right foot and push toward the left, stepping down on the ball of your left foot. Pull your right foot in toward you, keeping your feet slightly wider than shoulder width apart and your knees bent. Your weight is on the balls of your feet.

Slide step

The slide allows you to keep your opponent in front of you, and keep up with her, without standing up and pulling out of your defensive position (as you would have to do if you were running in a straight sprint). Coach Wescott points out that when you are sliding, your feet are never next to each other. "Take a six to eight inch step with one foot, and match that step with the other foot," she says.

Use the slide step in sync with the drop step.

Running Backward

One important footwork technique you will have to be comfortable with is running backwards. It sounds simple enough, but it is important for you to practice backpedaling. Lift your knees high as you move backwards down the field. Land and take off on the balls or your feet. Keep your weight centered in the middle of your body. If necessary, glance back over a shoulder to be sure you aren't heading for any obstacles. During a game situation, you will backpedal at short intervals. At times, you will have to gain some ground to keep the attack player you are marking in front of you—a quick and easy way to do this is to backpedal.

However, if you need to keep up with a sprinting attack player, or if she is passing you by, swivel your hips and point your feet in the direction you are running. Look over your shoulder at the attacker—it's easier to run forward

Running backward

than it is backward. Backpedaling is not a speed maneuver but a fast way to reposition your body in order to keep your attack player in front of you.

Steering Foot

Defenders also use a lead foot, or steering foot, in their stance. The steering foot is instrumental in directive defense. Directive defense is when a defender directs an attack player to one area of the field. The body positioning of a defender forces the offense to make a decision about where to move with the ball. As a defender, you must use this to your advantage and be aware of where you are at all times so that you can anticipate where the ball is going.

When marking an attack player, position your body so your back is to your goal. You want to keep the offender toward the outside of the field, far from the goal. If she is on your right, keep your left foot forward slightly so that your body interferes with her moving away from the sideline and into the middle of the field. If she is on your left, stand with your right foot forward slightly. The foot closest to the middle of the field is the steering foot, or the forward foot. Keep the offender on the opposite side of your steering foot toward the side of the field (the least dangerous area of the field). Keep your body in her path to the goal.

DRILLS AND GAMES

Wrist Strength

Players: One
Equipment: Lacrosse stick, timer

Stand straight with your feet shoulder width apart. Hold your lacrosse stick by the butt end with your right hand only. Hold your right arm straight out in front of you, with your elbow straight and your lacrosse stick extended in a straight line with your arm. Hold for one minute. Keep your arm straight in front of you, but rotate your wrist so the stick extends straight out to the left, parallel to the ground. Hold for one minute. Rotate your wrist again so the stick is straight out to the right. Hold for one minute. Rest and move the stick to your left hand and repeat this drill.

Repeat the above drill, but place a ball in the crosse when you hold it out in front of you. While you are holding the stick for one minute, continuously bounce the ball in the pocket of the stick. Keep your arm fully extended and your wrist flexed as you bounce.

Fancy Footwork

Players: Two
Distance: 25 yards

Stand facing your partner without your sticks. Put your hands on each other's shoulders. Your partner moves forward, running directly into you. She is working on offensive footwork—changing direction, changing speed, and stutter stepping as she moves forward down the field.

You are focusing on defensive footwork. When she moves forward, you start moving backward—start with a backpedal to get you going. However, you will soon notice that you lose speed when you backpedal. Practice slide stepping and drop stepping. Keep your upper body facing hers with your hands on her shoulders. Swivel your hips so your feet are moving in the same direction as your partner. Keep all your steps small and quick and lift your feet off the ground so you don't trip. Work hard for the entire 25-yard distance. Switch with your partner so you work on offensive footwork while she focuses on her defensive footwork.

Drop Step

Players: One
Distance: 25 yards

Start on the 25-yard line with your back to the end line of the field. Alternate drop stepping to the right and then to the left. Swing your hips to the side you are stepping back to and really drop your leg back. Cover the entire 25-yard distance doing nothing but drop stepping. Keep your knees bent and keep your weight on the balls of your feet and centered in the middle of your body. When you finish, jog back to the 25-yard line and repeat. Do this five times.

Zigzag Run

Players: One
Equipment: Five cones
Distance: 50 yards

Set up one cone on the 10-yard line in the middle of the field. From that cone, walk on a diagonal to the left to the 20-yard line and drop the second cone. From the second cone, walk on a diagonal to the right and drop the third cone on the 30-yard line so it is parallel with the cone on the 10-yard line. The fourth cone is on the 40-yard line and is parallel with the cone on the 20-yard line, and the fifth cone goes on the 50, parallel to the cone on the 30-yard line.

Start on the end line between the two lines of cones. Sprint hard on a diagonal to the first cone on the 10. As you approach, break down your steps. When you get to the outside of the cone, step down hard on your right foot and push off the outside of your right foot, changing direction toward the left. Sprint toward the second cone on the 20. When you approach the cone, break down your steps. When you reach the outside of the cone, step down hard on your left foot and push off the outside of your foot, stepping onto your right foot and heading to the right, to the third cone.

Practice breaking down your steps and changing direction at every cone. When you are finished, start over and incorporate a stutter-step at each cone. Change the direction after the stutter step. Include a body fake to really work on your offensive footwork.

W Slides

Players: One
Equipment: Five cones
Distance: 30-yard square

Set up five cones in a W formation. Place the first cone on the ground. Place the second cone on a diagonal line 10 yards away from the first. The third cone is on a diagonal line 10 yards away from the second, and parallel to the first cone. The fourth cone is diagonally 10 yards away from the third and parallel to the second cone, and the fifth cone is on a diagonal 10 yards away from the fourth and parallel to the first and third. Start at the top of the first cone standing in a low defensive stance. Your feet are slightly wider than shoulder-width apart, your knees are bent and your weight is on the balls of your feet. Hold your arms out to your sides with elbows bent toward the ground and palms facing out in front of you. Start with your right leg and shoulder facing the second cone, so you are looking into the W.

Slide step to the second cone, maintaining your balanced stance and keeping your feet equidistant as you slide. Remember, don't step too wide and don't pull your feet in right next to each other.

When you reach the second cone, pivot on the ball of your right foot, swinging your left leg to lead so it now faces the third cone. Your lead foot changes at every cone, however your upper body—the direction of your stance—does not change.

At the third cone, pivot on the ball of your left foot and swing your right leg around so it is leading to the fourth cone. Continue changing your lead foot at every cone until you complete the W. Repeat five times.

Suicide Sprints

Players: One
Distance: 100 yards

Stand on the end line of a 100-yard field. Sprint to the 25, bend down, and touch the 25-yard line. Pivot and sprint back to the end line, bend down, and touch the end line. Pivot and sprint to the 50-yard line, bend down, and touch the 50-yard line. Pivot and sprint back to the starting end line, bending down to touch the end line when you get there. Pivot again, sprint to the far 25-yard line and touch the line. Pivot and sprint back the 75 yards to the starting end line and touch the end line. Pivot and sprint 100 yards to the opposite end line and touch the end line. Pivot and make your final 100-yard sprint to the starting end line. Run through the end line; do not touch on your final sprint. Time yourself when you do this run. Aim to meet or increase your time whenever you do it.

Ladder Run

Players: One
Distance: 10 yards
Equipment: Chalk, tape, or rope

Mark off a distance of 10 yards. In that distance, create a "ladder" of one foot squares. One side of each square shares the same side with the square next to it until your row of one-foot squares covers the 10-yard distance. Create this ladder with tape if you're on a gym floor, or chalk or rope if you're outside on the grass.

Create a second ladder parallel to the first. Match the squares up so the two ladders mirror each other and are side by side, touching.

Start at one end of the 10 yards with each foot in front of a ladder. Your right foot will always only step into the right ladder, and your left foot will always only step into the left ladder. Never cross your feet over in front of each other during this drill.

Step with your right foot first into the first square of the right ladder. Lift your knee high and land on the ball of your foot in the square. Push off from the ball of your right foot and take a high knee step with your left leg, landing on the ball of your left foot in the second square on the left ladder.

Repeat this high stepping run until you move up the ladder and cross the 10 yard distance. This is a quick agility drill and is designed to get your feet moving in and out of tight spaces. Move as fast as you can, lifting your knees up high and only moving onto and off of the balls of your feet. Pump your arms as you run. Always stay within the grid you are stepping into. Try not to touch any lines.

Footwork Square

Players: One
Equipment: Four cones
Distance: Seven-yard square

Set up a seven-yard square with one cone in each corner. Start at the top left corner and drop step to the bottom left corner. Now sprint diagonally across the square to the top right corner. From there, backpedal to the bottom right corner. At the bottom right corner, slide step across to the bottom left corner. Sprint diagonally again to the top right corner. Now slide across the top of the square to the top left corner.

You are back where you started. Repeat your movements through the square seven times.

3

Individual Offense: Cradling & Dodges

THE BALL IS SNUG IN YOUR CROSSE. YOU WEAVE IN AND OUT OF YOUR opponents, moving first left, then right. You pull the crosse high and glance around the field, planning your next move. In one fluid movement, you roll off your defender and into an open space. You are one with your crosse and the ball. You are unstoppable.

Does this sound too good to be true? Well it's closer than you think. Although cradling may feel uncomfortable at first, it's like riding a bike—once you master it, it's a talent for life. The only way around feeling awkward is to practice, practice, and practice.

CRADLING

Your top arm—more specifically your wrist, fingers, and forearm—controls the cradling movement. Your lower arm is locked into place at your hip so the stick is on a diagonal. As your top hand moves the stick, the butt end of your stick twists in your bottom hand.

From the set position, push your fingers and rotate your wrist in toward your body so the stick head rotates toward your face. Continue moving the stick head in toward your body until the open side of the pocket faces the side of your head. Your forearm helps this movement, but as Coach Wescott points out, "Cradling is more hand and wrist than it is shoulder and elbow."

Flex your bottom wrist slightly away from your hips to allow the stick to move. Now cradle back into the set position by pulling the crosse back and behind your top shoulder. The stick head faces forward. Always contain the cradling movement to the top hand side of your body for protection from an oncoming check.

To maximize control when cradling, move your top hand up the stick closer to the stick head. However, if you want more mobility and flexibility in your cradle, slide your top hand down the shaft of the stick.

Good Form

Once you feel comfortable cradling in place, take it on the run. Start out slow and walk forward. Notice that the cradling motion of your arms falls into the natural rhythm of your body's movement as it travels forward. You must, however, fight the urge to move your arms back and forth, as you would in a straight run. While the rhythm is the same, the motion is slightly different. Pay careful attention to the movement of your top arm.

Always keep your head up when cradling the ball. It is imperative that you know where the defense is, where your open teammates are, and where the open space is when you have the ball. If your head is down or if you're staring at the ball in your crosse, you're missing opportunities to advance down the field. It is also your responsibility not to collide with the defense, something that is much more likely to happen if you're not watching where you're going.

The Ambidextrous Advantage

The stick does not stay locked in your left or right hand in lacrosse. You are constantly switching your top hand depending on where you are in relation to the defense, and where you are on the field.

When you first pick up a lacrosse stick, work through the mechanics of the cradle with your dominant hand on top. As soon as you have figured out the basic movement, switch your hands so your nondominant hand is on top. Become comfortable with the set position on your nondominant side. From the very beginning, learn to cradle with either hand and your offensive advantage will be tremendous. It is such an easy way to gain comfort on the field and succeed against your defense.

The best way to overcome any feeling of discomfort is to practice. Cradle for five minutes with your dominant hand on top, then switch positions and cradle for five minutes with your weaker hand. If you do this everyday, you will no longer have a "dominant" or "weaker" hand. They will be equal in strength when cradling.

Coach Wescott says, "I think the most exciting thing that I see is when a player is taught both hands up from the very beginning and it's great to see that more people can do everything with their left or right hand up. In fact," she continues, "we just call it stick side and nonstick side because then there's no idea of this is your strong hand or this is your weak hand."

Moving in the Set Position

Cradling isn't the only option for moving the ball down the field in your crosse. Another option is to run with the ball in the set position without actually cradling. Women's lacrosse is changing and developing similarities to the men's game. One such similarity is the lighter stick and deeper pocket. This allows players to move with the ball without having to cradle. With the crosse cocked at the top hand shoulder, a player is ready to pass, dodge, or shoot.

TRUNK FLEXIBILITY

As you work on your cradling skills, it is important to spend time developing flexibility in your upper body. In the beginning, you are focusing on the mechanics of the cradling movement. However, as you learn to cradle on the run, it is increasingly important for you to be flexible. Your trunk, or upper body, twists with every cradle. As you learn to switch hands in your cradle, you will need to be more flexible. Start stretching from the moment you start cradling, and it will be that much easier for you to adjust to the body movements associated with hand-switching and dodging. Important areas of your upper body to stretch before you begin cradling are your shoulders, upper arms, lower back, and obliques.

SWITCHING HANDS

Now you can cradle comfortably with either hand on top, but what happens in a game? You must be able to transition from one top hand cradle to the other without having to stop the game to readjust your hands. The goal is to switch hands seamlessly in mid-cradle, so the defender doesn't even realize exactly what has happened.

Switching hands is a necessary skill for dodging. It is, in effect, a dodge in itself. The mere action of changing your top hand is enough to alter the defense's perception of the ball and therefore give you yet another advantage. Keep the defense confused and unsure of your next move.

Full Cradle Swing and Switch

From the set position, swing your stick all the way across your body in a small semicircle to your lower hand side. Rotate the stick head in toward your body as you do when you cradle, but continue moving your top arm until your crosse is on your bottom hand side. The open pocket of the stick is fully rotated and facing forward. Your top hand grip is below the pocket of the stick, with the V formed by your thumb and forefinger underneath the open side of the pocket on the front of the stick. As you move the crosse, loosen your bottom hand grip until you complete the cradle. Once on your bottom hand side, tighten your lower hand. The stick is still on a diagonal, with the stick head out and to the outside of your bottom hand shoulder. Lead with your top shoulder to protect the crosse.

Once on the bottom hand side, slide your lower hand about halfway up the shaft of the stick. Adjust your hand so you grip the stick in the base of your fingers, with index finger extended up the shaft. Release your top hand and bring it down to the butt end, gripping the bottom of the stick. Keep the stick on a diagonal with the stick head off your shoulder. You are now in the set position on the opposite side from where you started. Switching sides is an incredibly important skill to learn. Coach Wescott points out that not enough players are switching sides: "Most people are picking a side and not moving across the head as much. They can see where the defender is trying to force them, and sometimes they just give in and cradle away from them. I think the attack players bow out too soon," she says.

As a general rule, change hands when you change feet. When you alter direction, change hands so your top hand matches the direction you're traveling in. This automatically positions your body so you can protect the ball with a lead shoulder.

CRADLING TO THE SIDE

Changing the direction of your cradle is an easy way to avoid an oncoming check and to give yourself extra time to determine your next move. Whenever you are feeling panicked on the field, cradle away from the defense and call for help. Listen to your teammates and look for either a passing option or an open space in which to move. Keep your eyes open and your head up so you can easily scan the field.

Left Cradle

If a defender approaches you on your right side, cradle to your left. It's common sense—whichever direction she's coming from, cradle to the opposite side. Just be sure that there is not another defender coming in on that side, too.

Start in the set position on the left side of your body. Twist your upper body to the left. Your left hand is on top of the stick and your right shoulder is leading. If your defender is coming from your right, this shoulder creates a natural barrier between her and the ball so your body is protecting your crosse. Cradling to the left is a natural way to make it more difficult for her to check your stick.

Right Cradle

If a defender is coming at you on the left side, cradle to the right with your right hand on top. Twist your upper body to the right with your left shoulder leading. Again, this creates a natural barrier between the defender and your crosse.

High Cradle

Another tactic to use when you need more time on the field is to cradle high. By pulling your body and your crosse up high, you move away from defenders and give yourself an extra second to think about your next move.

Imagine that you're walking down a crowded sidewalk with a friend. You pause next to a bench to tie your shoe. When you stand up, your friend is gone. How do you find her? Climb up on that bench so you have a better view of the sidewalk. From there, it is easy to spot your friend and easy to get her attention, too. The high cradle works the same way. Give yourself a moment to view the field and understand what your next best move is.

This cradle is slightly more difficult than the others because with more running speed, it is harder to keep the ball in the crosse. Straighten your body up so you have excellent posture. Extend your top arm so it is almost at full stretch above your head. The cradling action stays the same. Pay special attention to your top arm. There is a tendency for the top elbow to tuck into the stick. This is a surefire way for the ball to fall out of the crosse. Keep your top wrist flexed and your top elbow pointing out away from your body. Keep the stick on a slight diagonal with your lower arm.

When you lift the stick up above your head, the pocket naturally leans back over your head. This is what makes this move so difficult. The pocket is leaning toward the ground, and gravity dictates that the ball will fall out and onto the ground. If you have enough speed in your cradle, and if your motions are smooth and the mechanics are perfect, you will not have a problem losing the ball.

OFFENSIVE ADVICE

As an offensive player, never go into any situation with a set plan of action. The defender is going to position herself to dictate your play. To a certain extent, you must acknowledge her positioning and react to that. She may eliminate the very dodge you were planning on doing. However if you have a pocket full of options, you'll be able to get around her no matter where she is.

Always enter the situation ready to assess your options and move in the best direction. Be ready for any dodge. The sport is very free flowing and unrestricting. Planning too much takes away from that, and impedes your progress offensively.

DODGES

Every player, regardless of position, should master dodging. Both offensive and defensive players can use dodging effectively. For instance, an offensive player headed for the goal can dodge around a defender to get in position to pass or take a shot. Likewise, a defensive player can use a dodge to clear the ball from her end and deny the opposition a scoring opportunity.

Speed and quickness are essential in dodging. But they aren't the only requirements. Effective dodgers use head and shoulder fakes to get the opponent off balance. Players can also move the stick from one hand to the other or quickly raise or lower it. Remember, you only need to create a split second of confusion in the defender's mind to get past her. You want your opponent to "bite" at one of your moves and get off balance. Then you can quickly pass her by. You must keep your balance too. If you lunge to get past your opponent, you can easily slip or fall and lose your advantage.

In dodging, you must improvise. You can't have a set movement in mind when the defender approaches. You must watch her eyes and movements, then quickly assess your best strategy for getting past her. Always remember to move up the field toward the goal, not simply side to side. And always protect the ball. Keep your stick close to your body or your opponent can knock the ball loose with her stick.

One-Handed Dodge

When you come face to face with a defender, an easy way to move around her is to drop your top hand and sprint past her keeping your body between her and your stick. When you drop your top hand, the bottom hand takes control of the stick. Hold the stick parallel to the ground and away from the defender. Slightly cock your lower wrist so the ball stays in the crosse. Dropping the top hand allows you to maintain your maximum speed by using that free arm to pump while you run. There is no significant cradle movement when running one handed. Use this burst of speed to move quickly past the defense.

If you move into an open space and are headed for a fast breakaway, continue with one hand on the stick to keep your speed up. But only continue this move if you are positive no one is around you. The action gets you down the field faster. However, once you move back into a crowded area, or if a defender catches up with you, return the top hand to the stick and control your cradle. You are less likely to survive a stick check with only one hand on your crosse.

Remember, too, that it is a foul to use a free hand to ward off the defense. Placing your free arm back on the stick ensures that it doesn't wander out and push away any oncoming defense.

Stutter-Step Dodge

The stutter-step dodge is also referred to as a face-on dodge. As the name indicates, you are facing your defender when you execute this dodge. It is a combination of footwork techniques, body fakes, and cradling skill. Use the stutter-step dodge to move around a defender into an open space. Always look for an opportunity to use a dodge to move into the open space and then either shoot on goal or pass to a teammate. As you approach a defender, determine if you want to move around her to the left or to the right. Prepare for this move by checking that your top hand matches the direction you plan to move in. If you are heading to the right, your right hand is your top hand.

When you approach the defender, break down your steps so you are in control of your body and your crosse.

Let's imagine you plan on moving past the defender to the right. Come face-to-face with the defender and stutter step to the right, cradling the crosse to the right of your body. Stutter step means you take a quick, short half step to the right, pumping your upper body in that direction. Push off your left foot and stutter step to the right with your right foot. Focus on upper body fakes—pump your shoulders and upper body as you stutter step. Quickly step back again on your left foot before exploding off your left foot again toward the right. Lead with your left shoulder to protect your stick.

It is also possible to stutter step in the opposite direction you intend to explode past the defender. For example, stutter step to the right and then explode past the defender to the left. Regardless of which direction you go, the shoulder closest to the defender is leading so it protects your crosse. Twist your upper body away from the defender in addition to protect your crosse.

This dodge relies on your quick change of direction, footwork and your body fake. You have the advantage of moving forward, while your defender is facing you, so she will have to be moving backward. Right away, this indicates that you will be successful in this confrontation, assuming that you are in control of your body and stick movements. You must move with confidence and grace.

Roll Dodge with Hand Change

The roll dodge is a great dodge to use when you need to create space. Decide first which way you want to move around the defender. This is a great dodge if you are in the 12-meter fan and closing in on goal space. A shift such as a roll dodge creates enough space for you to get away from your defender and shoot on goal.

Right Roll Dodge

To execute a right roll dodge, first approach the defender on a diagonal, keeping her on your right. Protect the cradle by cradling on your left, with your left hand up. As she shifts over to mark you and possibly execute a stick check, plant your right foot on the outside of her right foot. Pivot away from the defender off the ball of your right foot. Drop your left leg back and swing your hips to the back of the field so your back is to the defender. Continue moving in this circular motion. Plant your left foot down and pivot on the ball of your left foot, swinging around so you are once again facing forward, but now on the right of the defender.

As you make this final pivot, switch cradling hands. Slide your bottom right hand up and drop your left hand down to the bottom of the stick. Cradle to the right with your left shoulder leading and protecting your crosse. Explode off your left foot and move around the defender on the right.

Left Roll Dodge

To roll dodge to the left, approach the defender on a diagonal to the right, so she is on your left. Cradle to the right with your right hand on top of the stick. When she shifts to mark you, plant your left foot outside her left foot. Pivot off the ball of your left foot away from the defender toward the back of the field. Swing your right leg back so your body turns in a semicircle motion. Plant your right foot so your hips are now facing the back of the field and your back is to the defender. Pivot off your right foot. Keep your weight on the ball of your foot as you turn. Complete the circle by swinging your left leg around and planting it so your left toe is facing forward. Explode off your right foot and sprint past the defender on the left side.

When you make the final pivot off your right foot (when your back is to the defender) switch hands on your cradle. Slide your left hand up and drop your right hand so it is now on the bottom of the stick. When you finish your pivot, cradle on the left side of your body with your left hand on top.

Your right shoulder is leading and creating a natural barrier between your crosse and the defender.

BODY LANGUAGE AND FOOTWORK

The final component to a successful offensive player is confidence in body language and footwork. None of the above dodges or cradling maneuvers will be of much use to you if your feet and your body aren't working in sync with your cradle. If you attempt to dodge to the left, but neglect to fake right first, you essentially are giving your defense the go ahead that you're about to dodge.

Focus on quick feet and small steps with your weight on the balls of your feet. Keep your heels up and your knees bent, and you're ready to roll in any direction.

DRILLS AND GAMES

Cradle Race

Players: Two or more
Equipment: Sticks and balls
Distance: 25 yards

Stand next to one teammate on the end line. Each player has a ball in her crosse. At the same time, start cradling on the run to the 25-yard line. If you drop the ball out of your crosse, pick it up and take two steps backward before cradling forward to the 25 again. The first player to the 25 wins the race. As you progress with this contest, time yourself and race against yourself.

Mirror Image

Players: Two
Equipment: Stick

Stand facing your partner, one stick length away from her. You and your partner hold your sticks in the set position without the ball. Your partner begins cradling in any direction she chooses, and you mirror her cradle. If she cradles on her left side, you cradle on your right. Your feet are stationary in this drill; there is no movement other than cradling. For three minutes mirror your partner's action. Watch her movements and be aware of her cradling technique. Is her stick head back near her top hand shoulder? Is her stick on a diagonal? After three minutes, rest and tell her what you noticed. Let her know if she did a good job too. Start again. This time you direct the cradle and she mirrors your image. Pay special attention to the mechanics of your move, how you switch hands when you alter your cradle. She will notice everything you do, so make sure you do it right!

Stick Work Strength

Players: One
Equipment: Stick and ball

Start in the set position and cradle back to your top hand side. Hold the crosse so the open pocket is facing away from your body, with the back of the pocket facing your shoulder. With your bottom hand, twist the stick away from your body (if your right hand is the bottom, twist counterclockwise; if the left hand is on bottom, twist clockwise). Move the stick with the fingers of your lower hand. When the pocket rotates around so you can see the ball and the open side is facing you, tighten your top grip and with your top hand fingers finish the full rotation so the stick is back in the starting position. Your bottom hand and top hand are working together to complete one full rotation with the stick. Continue this move for five minutes, and then switch top hands and rotate to the other side. This will increase your wrist and finger strength.

Zigzag Swap

Players: One
Equipment: Five cones, stick, ball
Distance: 50 yards

Set up the cones on the field in a zigzag format. Place the first cone in the middle of the field on the 10-yard line. Place the second cone on the 20-yard line diagonally left of the first cone. Place the third cone on the 30-yard line and directly in line with the first cone. Place the fourth cone on the 40-yard line and directly in line with the cone on the 20-yard line. The fifth cone goes on the 50-yard line and is lined up with the cones on the 30- and the 10-yard lines.

Start at the end line between the two lines of cones. Cradle while you run on a diagonal to the right to the outside of the 10-yard line cone. Cradle on your right side with your right hand on top since you are running to the right. When you reach the outside of the first cone, cut in toward the second cone and run on a diagonal to the left to the outside of the 20 yard cone. When you make this cut and change direction, remember to switch hands on your stick. Your left hand is on top of the stick and your cradle is to the left of your body. Continue this zigzag motion down the field until you reach the last cone.

Roll Away

Players: Two
Equipment: Sticks and one ball
Distance: 10 yards

In this drill, one player is a dummy defender (more positively referred to as a cooperative defender) and the second player is the offender. Start as the offender on the end line. The cooperative defender stands five yards away in a defensive stance with her stick out in front of her. This defender cannot actively pursue the ball and stick check. She must stand still in a defensive stance with her stick out in front of her.

You are the attack player on the end line with the ball in your crosse. Cradle forward toward the defender. In your first move past the defender, execute a right roll dodge. Run on a diagonal to your left (using a left side cradle) and roll off the defender, exploding past her on the right. Be sure to change speed when you approach and move away from the defender.

Once you successfully pass her, approach again but this time execute a left roll dodge. Do two of each dodges and then switch roles.

Creative Dodging Contest

Players: Six
Equipment: Sticks and balls

This is a fun, creative contest. Three players compete for most creative dodge, and three players act as judges. Judge scores on a scale from one to five, five being the highest score.

Each competitor stands before the group with a crosse and ball, and goes up against another competitor, acting strictly as a cooperative defender (the defender does NOT try to get the ball from the attack player). One by one, the competitors execute a dodge that they have made up. It can be any combination of footwork, body fakes, and hand changing dodge—anything that gets the attack player past the defender. At the end of each dodge, the judges reveal their scores. The three judges cannot consult each other before revealing their scores.

Have fun and be creative! Don't be afraid to explore any options. This is a fun way to figure out your attack style.

Grounded Attack

Players: Two
Equipment: Sticks and ball

One attack player starts with the ball in her crosse. A defender starts in front of her. When the game starts, the defender is free to move around the attack player however she wants. Her goal is to get the ball. She can come from ahead, behind, or either side. She cannot execute any illegal stick checks, but she is free to move in any direction. The attack player, on the other hand, must keep one foot on the ground at all times. She can pull the crosse to either side (away from the defender) to protect the ball. She can twist her upper body and pivot around off her stationary foot, however she must keep the ball of that stationary foot on the ground at all times. Play for one minute and switch roles.

How Many Fingers?

Players: Three
Equipment: Four cones, one stick, ball
Distance: Five-yard grid

Set up a five-yard square with one cone in each corner. Each grid holds one attack player with the ball and one defender. The object is for the attack player to move across the square using cradling and dodging techniques to move past the defender. The defender does not have a stick, but is working on body positioning and footwork. While the attack player tries to cradle to a side or dodge around the defender, the defender is slide stepping, drop stepping and backpedaling to keep the attack in front of her and to prevent her from moving forward.

The catch: While all this is going on, a third player is standing outside of the square to either side. This player holds up any number of fingers.

The attack player must look up at this third player as she moves across the grid and call out how many fingers the third player is holding up. If she calls out the wrong number, or if she never looks up, the defender gets a point. If she moves around the defense while looking up and calls out the right number, she gets a point.

For five minutes work in the same positions. If the attack moves across the grid successfully, she turns around and comes back the other way. The third player keeps track of each player's points.

After five minutes rotate positions. Continue until all players have completed each role.

Cradle Weave

Players: One
Equipment: Five cones, stick and ball
Distance: Four yards

Create a four-yard square with one cone in each corner. Place the fifth cone in the middle of the square. Start at one corner and cradle into the center cone. Dodge around the cone and change directions, moving out to a different corner cone than the one you started from. Continue weaving through the cones, changing your direction, speed and cradling techniques as you go. At each cone, practice a roll dodge, switch cradling hands, or pull the stick to your reverse side. Change your speed and direction in sync with your cradling moves.

This movement is free flowing, you can move through the square however you want. The important thing is to incorporate all of your footwork and stick work techniques as you go. This drill encourages free thinking and creativity, which will help you out when you come face to face with a defender.

4

Individual Defense

WHEN YOU WERE A CHILD, DID YOU EVER TRY TO OUTRUN YOUR SHADOW? If not, go outside in your backyard the next time the sun is shining. Turn so your back is to the sun and your shadow falls on the ground in front of you. For 10 minutes, try to get away from your shadow. You will soon notice that no matter what you do, your shadow is always right there on the ground in front of you.

Individual defense in lacrosse is based on the shadow theory. Due to the positioning of the teams on the field at the start of the game, the defensive nature of the game is player-to-player. This means that you have one girl to mark, or guard, and you stay with her no matter what.

By the end of this chapter, you will learn how to be your attack player's shadow. By learning different defensive positioning and checks, you will stop your attacking opponent from advancing down the field and, more importantly, from scoring a goal. Defense dictates the way offense plays, so play with authority and know your power.

MARKING

Marking is guarding a player in player-to-player style defense. Always face your attack player with your back to the goal you are defending. You never want your mark to be closer to your defensive goal than you are. This is how goals are scored. As a defender, your main goal is to prevent the other team from scoring. However, you're also looking to cause turnovers and start an offensive fast break. During a game, you will mark players who have the ball and players who do not. When an offensive player doesn't have the ball and is far from the ball carrier, you can back off. But don't lose your concentration. Watch the action intently. As soon as your opponent catches a pass or nears the ball carrier, you need to tighten your coverage.

If your opponent has the ball, look to block or intercept a pass. Keep her from running where she wants. Direct her toward other defenders or away from the center of the field where she has fewer passing and scoring chances. When guarding a player, keep your feet and shoulders virtually square to the ball carrier, but position yourself slightly to her side. Learn to take short, lateral steps to stay close to the ball carrier. Don't let her get past you.

Pretend there is an imaginary line that starts at the center of your defensive goal and ends at your attacking opponent. Typically, the opponent will be toward one side of the field or the other, so the line will be on a diagonal. Stand along this diagonal line between the attack player and the goal. Angle your body toward the side of the field where the attack is. Your inside foot, or the foot closest to the middle of the field, is slightly ahead of your body. This angle keeps you positioned with your opponent in front of you and your back to the goal. Because you are slightly toward the middle of the field, your presence also keeps the attack player away from the middle of the field and closer to the sideline.

Judging Distance

An important step to playing good defense is the ability to judge your distance from both your attacking player and the ball. When marking a player, you want to be no more than one stick length away from her. In fact, it is illegal to be farther than one stick length away from your mark for more than three seconds when inside your defensive eight-meter arc. This is a major foul.

To remain within one stick length of your opponent, you must use the defensive footwork discussed in Chapter 2: sliding, drop stepping, sprinting, and backpedaling.

CHECKING

There are two different types of checks in women's lacrosse: body checking and stick checking. Do not confuse either one with the checks in the men's game. Men's lacrosse is very rough and involves a lot of body contact. Although the term *body checking* is used in women's lacrosse, it refers to the actual defensive positioning of the body on the field in

relation to the attack player. Remember, there is no body contact at all in the game. The most contact you make with another player is when you execute a stick check.

BODY CHECKING

The term *body checking* does not refer to slamming your opponent into the ground and causing her to lose possession of the ball as she falls into the mud. In women's lacrosse, body checking is a way of positioning yourself to slow down the ball carrier. Essentially, it is good defensive positioning.

In the beginning of this chapter, you were asked to go into your backyard to try to escape from your shadow. You soon realized that this is an impossible task. When body checking, you are your opponent's shadow. Stick with her no matter what—just like your shadow does to you.

When to Body Check

Imagine an attack player gets the ball at midfield and is moving toward the goal. She has an open path to the net. As a good defender, you know that you can't let her get away with an unobstructed route to goal.

The first step in executing a body check is to take note of a situation as described above. An attack player with the ball is moving toward the goal, and no one is slowing her down. The second step is reacting to that type of situation. Position yourself between the attack player and the goal and become the much-needed obstacle in her path. How you position your body dictates the direction the attack player goes. If possible, always force her to her bottom hand side.

When stepping into this path, remember to give the attacker enough time to realize you are there and plan an alternate course. If you jump out in front of her as she is running past you, the ref will call a blocking foul on you. Set yourself up so she can see you and knows that she must pass or dodge around you. If she does run right into you, a charging foul will be called on her.

> ### PLAY SMART
>
> At the start of the game, take time to notice your attack player's top hand. Usually, her dominant hand is her top hand. As you position yourself to body check your attack player, use this knowledge to your advantage. If she is running down the middle of the field, body check her toward her bottom hand side and force her to abandon her dominant cradling side.

Body Positioning

Balance is key to good defensive positioning. Stand with your feet slightly wider than shoulder width apart and bend your knees. Center your weight on the balls of your feet and lean forward slightly. In this position, you are ready to move in any direction. Do not bend at the waist and lean forward. Coach Wescott points out that defenders sometimes do this when they are tired. Leaning forward takes you off balance and out of good positioning, which allows the attacker to move past you.

Stand in front of the attack player you are guarding with your back to the goal in the marking position. Stand square to the attacking player. Square means that the middle of your chest is centered with whichever part of her is closest to goal.

Imagine the following scenario: The attacker is toward the right side of the field. You position yourself on the imaginary marking line, so you are in front of her and slightly toward the middle of the field, which is your left. Your left foot is slightly ahead of your right. If she is positioned so she is facing straight toward the end line, you are square to her right shoulder since that shoulder is closest to you, and therefore closest to goal.

By standing more toward the middle of the field, yet angled out to face her, you are causing your opponent to stay to the sideline and away from the middle of the field and the goal. This is called concealing, or containing, your player. This slows her down and removes her from a potentially threatening position.

Stick Positioning

From the set position, move your stick out in front of you in a vertical position. Slide your top hand about halfway down the shaft to increase your defensive reaching distance. Your top hand is in front of your face and the stick head extends up into the air with the open pocket facing forward. Extend your top arm out toward your opponent so the stick head is at a 45-degree angle to the ground. Move your lower hand off your hip, but keep the butt end of the stick close to your midsection so the stick head is angled down toward the ground.

Holding your stick upward and angled down broadens your defensive positioning. The attack player is forced to react to the farthermost part of your extended body—the pocket of your stick. This, in turn, gives you time to react to her moves. Instead of her attempting to dodge or change direction when she is right in your face (which is more difficult for you because you don't have time to react), she now must make a move sooner—at your stick.

Keep your crosse on the inside of her stick to prevent her from cutting inside and moving toward the middle of the field and on to goal. Keeping her outside toward the nearest sideline ensures that she is not in a position to close in on goal.

Footwork

A still defender is a useless one. "Once you put the stick in [a defender's] hands, she thinks defense is more with the stick, and it's not. Eighty to ninety percent of defense is with your feet," says Coach Wescott.

If you are standing still, your opponent will simply run around you. All of your good positioning work will go to waste. Keep your knees bent with your weight forward on the balls of your feet. Always keep your feet moving, and take small, quick steps. The most important part about defense is being in the right position, and quick footwork gets you there.

As the attack player approaches, begin backpedaling. Small decisive backpedals keep you moving so you gain momentum and can keep up with her. As you continue to move with her, swivel your hips so your feet are moving in the same direction she is, while your upper body is still square to her.

STEERING

Following your body check, decide whether you want to steer a player in a certain direction or execute a stick check. Coach Wescott advises, "Body position is more important than checking. You never want to lose position to get possession." In other words, steer her away from goal before thinking about stick checking.

Steering is often used when you are up against an advanced ball carrier. If there is a fear that you will strike your opponent instead of her stick, do not attempt to check. In this situation, it is better to steer the attack player toward the side of the field and keep her far away from goal. Eliminate her passing options and run her into a corner so she has no chance of scoring a goal. Again, as in body checking, know which side you want to steer your opponent to. Always try to move her toward her bottom hand side. Do not, however, steer her across the middle of the field in an effort to get her to her weak side. This is dangerous because the middle of the field has more offensive options than the side. There is more room for dodges or passes.

Body Positioning

Steering is a continuation of body checking on the run. After body checking a player, continue steering her to her weak side and keep her on the outside of the field. Keep your upper body square to your opponent, as you did when body checking. Swivel your hips so your legs are running with your opponent in the direction you are steering her. Maintain the one stick length distance from her. Lead with the shoulder that you are steering her toward. If you are forcing her to your left, your left shoulder is diagonally in line with your left defensive corner of the field.

Stick Positioning

Hold your stick in the barrier position. A barrier position actually creates a horizontal "wall" through which the attack player cannot go. As you move with her, hold your stick horizontally in front of you. Do not change your grip, but just drop your top arm and raise your bottom arm so the stick is parallel to the ground. The pocket of your stick falls on either side of the ball carrier, depending on which side you are steering your opponent toward and which hand was your top hand.

Continue moving on the diagonal line, forcing your attacker to the outside of the field. Position your body so the cradler can neither go straight forward, nor can she pull back and cut inside of you. Because you are moving with her and your stick is extended in such a fashion, you are preventing her from doing anything but continuing along this diagonal path. Do not touch your opponent with your stick in any way. If you are physically forcing her toward the side with your stick, the ref will call a holding foul on you.

Do not attempt to stick check the ball carrier. Steering is all about guiding the cradler. If you step toward her in an effort to stick check, you commit to her and come out of your defensive positioning, giving her an opportunity to sprint around you.

> ## WORDS TO LIVE BY
>
> **"I try to teach my players to enjoy the opportunity they have in competition. Someone else is there not just to play against you and beat you down, but they're there to teach you to be a better player. The better they are, the more they challenge you and the better chance you have of learning more because they're going to make you reach your peak performance. Even though you're playing against somebody, there's a dance between the two of you, and a cooperation between the two of you—you're learning and working together."**
>
> —Denise Wescott
> Delaware University head coach

STICK CHECKING

There are times when you can successfully stick check your opponent to get the ball. If the attack is in a shooting position, stick check (if you can without reaching across her body). If the attack isn't protecting her crosse, go for the stick check. You can only execute a stick check when your opponent has the ball in her crosse. If you check an empty stick, the ref will call a minor foul on you.

A stick check is a series of controlled taps against your opponent's stick in an attempt to dislodge the ball from her crosse. The actual stick checking motions are short, sharp movements that stem from your top wrist.

Hold the stick so you are in a good body checking position. Slide your top hand about halfway down the stick. If you feel you are not in control of your checking movement, move the top hand up closer to the pocket. A higher top hand provides greater control, however, lowering that hand gives you more leverage and a farther reach.

When you stick check, reach out to your opponent's stick and flick your top wrist forward. With your bottom hand, pull the butt end of the stick down as you snap your top wrist forward. The bottom hand acts as a lever, propelling the pocket of the stick forward. Move your arms in sync so your stick taps down and away from your opponent's face in a smooth and strong motion. Do not pull your stick head back first before going for the check. "Sometimes players dip back and take a back swing before they check. Players should just take the top hand to the check and use the bottom hand to pull the bottom of the stick in," says Coach Wescott.

CHECKING FROM BEHIND

As a guide, check your feet in relation to your opponent's feet to determine when and how to check. Your feet must always be moving in the same direction as your opponent's in order to safely stick check.

If your feet are behind hers and you are running behind your opponent, you are only allowed to back check. A back check is executed from behind the attacking player. Her stick, however, must be out to the side of her body. You are legally permitted to attempt a back check *only* if you can see your opponent's stick extending to the side. Again, do not reach across any part of her body to check. But if the stick is out to the side, stick check away from her body.

Tap the pocket of your opponent's stick with the upper corner of the head of the stick. Tap two or three times in a series, and then quickly retreat to the body checking position. If you follow through on your check and don't retreat to your defensive position, the ref will call a holding foul on you. This is a major foul.

Create a rhythm of taps that you are comfortable with, for example: tap-tap-tap-retreat. Repeat this series of tapping motions until the ball is dislodged from her stick. Do not swing your crosse at your opponent. Always use controlled, small tapping motions—never one long swoop—to get at the ball.

Remember, every player has a seven-inch bubble around her head, within which no other stick can go. Make sure your opponent's stick is away from her face. Your checking motion must always move away from her head.

Never reach across your opponent's body in an attempt to stick check. This is illegal. If she is carrying her crosse away from you, work on your body positioning and do not stick check.

One important thing to remember about stick checking is that you may not always dislodge the ball on the first try. This does not mean that you are unsuccessful in your check, though. The goal of a stick check is to disrupt the cradling rhythm of the attack player. Even if the ball doesn't come loose, you are frustrating and aggravating your opponent, and this means success for you. You are interfering with the attack player's concentration. Distracted and frustrated, she will easily lose control of the ball.

Generally, you want to be in front of the ball carrier or slightly to her side to attempt a stick check. However, you may also stick check from behind. But you cannot reach across the offensive player's body. Your stick cannot come near her head. Usually, you won't succeed in knocking the ball loose on your first stick check, regardless of your position. But stay under control and make short taps on her stick. Keep your feet moving. Be prepared when the ball does fall to the ground so you can scoop it up.

> ### UPWARD CHECK ON GROUND BALLS
>
> As your skill progresses, you will execute more advanced checks. One such stick check is the upward check. Use this check when your opponent is picking up a ground ball. In this check, the tapping action of your stick is actually an upward motion. By hitting your opponent's stick on an upswing, you dislodge the ball from her pocket and send it up into the air. From there, you are free to extend your stick and catch the ball, pulling it into yourself to cradle and transition to offense.
>
> Disclaimer: This move is more advanced because the motion of your stick is slightly more dangerous. If you do not have great control and balance, you risk hitting your opponent in the face. Not only is this unsuitable and dangerous for play, but it will also get you kicked out of a game. Only attempt this check after much practice.

Practice

To practice a stick check, hang a piece of string from the ceiling. Defensively position yourself in front of the string. Pretend the string is your opponent's stick. Start in a good body checking position, then reach out and with a snap of your top wrist and a pull of your lower arm, move your stick in a quick tapping motion down and away through the part of the string that you are checking.

INTERCEPTION

One of the best ways to change the pace of the game and transition from defense to offense is to intercept the ball. An interception occurs when you, as a defender, anticipate a pass the opposing team is about to make. You step into the line of the pass to catch the ball before the intended recipient has a chance to do so.

Interception is all about judging distance and timing. Sometimes, it is very obvious where and when a player is going to pass. However, if you advance into that pathway too soon, you give the passer a chance to go for another option. When you intercept, always wait until the last minute and then accelerate onto the line of the pass. Move quickly onto the ball so you cut off the intended recipient. Once you gain possession, accelerate again out of the situation. Don't stop to pat yourself on the back for a job well done or the opposing team will be all over you in a matter of seconds. Continue quickly moving away from the scene of the interception, and look to pass to an open teammate.

One-Handed Reach

Often times, when an interception occurs, it is a one-handed catch or a knock down. No matter what, keep your eyes on the ball as you move onto the pass. If you can catch it or knock it down with two hands on your stick, do so. If necessary, extend the stick with a one-handed grip to extend your reach. If the pass is coming from your left, hold the stick with only your right hand to reach out for the ball. If the pass is coming from your right, hold the stick with your left hand only.

BLOCKING

The other side of interception is blocking. While interception occurs before the ball reaches the intended recipient, blocking occurs as the ball leaves the passer's stick. As a defender, you must know where and when the ball is leaving your opponent's stick. Again, you have to anticipate the action, but don't give it away if you know it because this gives the passer a chance to change her mind.

You are facing the ball carrier and have defensively eliminated her movement options on the field so she is forced to pass. Stay square to her and keep your weight low and on the balls of your feet. Bend your knees. Keep your eyes on the ball and on your opponent's eyes. Be prepared to extend your stick vertically to block shots. Blocking requires close marking, balance, patience, and a lot of control. You cannot move too soon. Your stick is out in front of you, impeding your opponent's progress as she glances around the field for someone to pass to. Your pocket is near her face, either open side or back side facing her. For this defensive play, it does not matter which way the pocket is facing, as long as one flat side is facing her.

This move is not a check. As she attempts to make her pass, line your stick up with the passer and then extend your stick above her stick. In this position, your stick covers the pathway of the ball. Knock the ball down, then scoop it up and continue on to an offensive transition.

RECOVERY

Occasionally, although you have perfected your body checking position, an attack player might slip by you. What do you do? Recover. When an attack player passes you, turn around and sprint to catch up with her. The worst thing you can do as a defender is sigh, hang your head, and turn around to watch the attack player continue her streak down the field. That's no way to play this sport! Hold your head high, turn around, and make it up!

Sprint down the field, taking the straightest path toward the goal. Stay on the inside of the attacker, keeping her on the outside of the field. Once again, your body positioning dictates what she is able, and not able, to do. As you run, extend your crosse in front of you to distract her. Do not hit her, swat at her stick, or attempt to knock the ball from her in any way. Rather, hold your stick with one arm just as a guide. When you overtake her, and you will overtake her, approach from the inside of the field. Steer her toward the outside and slow her down, moving her away from the goal.

DRILLS AND GAMES

Leader of the Pack

Players: 10
Equipment: 10 crosses, five balls, mouthguards
Distance: 12-meter fan

Divide the group of 10 into two groups: five attack players and five defensive players. The attack players each get a ball. Everyone starts inside the 12-meter fan. No one is allowed to leave the fan. All attack players must be cradling at all times. The defensive players move around the circle, attempting to stick check the attack players. All check movements are down and away from the attack players' faces.

Attack players work on tight, controlled cradling, while the defenders are moving into proper position to stick check and dislodge the ball. When an attack player loses the ball, she must leave the fan. When a defender attempts three stick checks in a row and does not once dislodge the ball, she must leave the fan. If a defender misses twice but gets the ball on the third attempt, her slate is clean to start over with three strikes again.

The last player remaining in the circle represents her team of offense or defense, and is the leader of the pack. Switch teams and play again.

Body Positioning

Players: Two
Distance: Eight-meter arc

Start at the top of the eight-meter arc. The attack player is facing the goal and the defender has her back to the goal. The attack player is attempting to get close to the crease, and the defender's job is to keep her out. This is all about body positioning. The attack player stutter steps, rolls, changes speed and direction in an effort to move past the defender. She cannot charge into the defender. The defender is drop stepping, sliding, and backpedaling, and always keeping the attack directly in front of her. She is square to the attack with her back to the goal.

Play for one minute. If the attack player makes it to the crease line, she gets one point. If the defender keeps her out of the crease, she receives one point. After each minute of play, rest for 30 seconds. Repeat three times in the same roles, and then switch positions so each player has a chance to be attack and defense.

Positioning with Crosse

Players: Two
Equipment: Two sticks
Distance: 25 yards

Stand facing your partner, about five yards away from her. Stand in a good defensive position, with your weight low and your knees bent. Hold your crosse up high in front of you in a defensive stance. Hold your stick with a firm grip, but keep your arms relaxed. Your partner is the attack player. She moves toward you, going through the motions of cradling (but without the ball), working on her footwork. Move with your partner, keeping your feet moving and keeping your offensive player in front of you. Work on your body checking position. Hold your crosse up high and in front of your opponent. Always keep her stick on the outside, so your stick is on the inside, closer to the center of the field. Be sure to keep your stick away from her head and body. Do not attempt to stick check. When the attack player crosses over the 25 yards, switch roles and play again.

Recovery

Players: Two
Equipment: Sticks and ball
Distance: 30 yards

An offensive player starts at the 25-yard line with a ball, facing the end line. The defender starts behind the attack player at the 30-yard line, also facing the end line. At the count of three, the attack player sprints toward the goal, cradling as she goes. The defender also starts sprinting in an effort to catch the runaway attack player. In this recovery move, the defender must run straight toward goal on the inside of the attack player, forcing the player toward the outside of the field. When she regains her defensive positioning, the defender steers the attacker away from the goal toward the closest sideline.

Tap Tap Tap

Players: Two
Equipment: Two sticks, mouthguards

One teammate is the dummy, or cooperative offensive player. She stands still in body positioning, but cradles as if she has the ball. You are her defender. Neither you nor your teammate move your feet in this drill. As she cradles, stick check her. Start in the body check position, facing your opponent and tap-tap-tap then retreat to your body check position. Check that your tapping check motions are all down and away from your teammate's face. Switch roles.

5

Passing and Receiving

Passing is the heart of the women's lacrosse game. Unlike the men's game, there is no body contact, no checking, and no excessive roughness. The flow of the game lies in passing. "You play with 12 people on the field, so you must be accurate in your feeds—it's one of the most important things," says Coach Wescott.

The important thing to remember about passing is the other end of it: receiving. A pass is only as good as its reception. If the ball is thrown off target, or if the receiver is not comfortable catching the pass, then your team gets nowhere. You must not only understand how to throw the ball and when to use different throws in different situations, but also how to receive the ball.

PASSING

Effective passes are critical because they advance the ball much more quickly down the field than having to run with the ball. The quicker you get the ball near the goal, the quicker you can shoot. A team of good passers will get many more shots than a poor shooting team. Passing is a difficult skill to master. It's easy to overthrow or underthrow your teammate or miss them to the left or right. Bad passes often result in turnovers. But be patient. Keep practicing, work on the correct fundamentals, and you can become an excellent passer. To understand how important and efficient passing is, stand next to a teammate. Have a third teammate stand 20 yards away. All three of you have your crosses, and you and the teammate next to you each have a ball. On the count of three, sprint to your third teammate, cradling the ball as you go. At the same time, your teammate next to you throws her ball to the third teammate at the 20-yard mark. See which ball gets there first—the one your teammate threw, or the one you are running with as you cradle. Time this exercise and see by how much the ball beats you—a significant difference in a game where every second counts!

Ideally, passes are executed from a set, standing position. This gives you more time to make an accurate pass. However, players are always on the move during a lacrosse game. You can rarely stand perfectly still when you pass. Instead, you're usually dodging defenders to find an opening. Pass quickly before defenders close in and try to block the ball. In addition, learn to lead your teammate, or throw the ball in front of her. She isn't standing still either. If you throw the ball at her while she's running, it will land behind her. Instead, you need to throw it in front of her and let her run to the ball without breaking stride. It's always better to overthrow, rather than underthrow your teammate. A pass that falls short can easily be scooped up by the defense and turned into a quick goal.

There are many different types of passing, each of which will be addressed in this chapter. Regardless of the style of pass, Coach Wescott offers the following advice: "Using both hands really gives you more power. Getting the technique of snapping the top wrist and pulling the bottom arm is so important."

Overhand Pass/Shoulder Pass

The overhand pass, or shoulder pass, uses the same body movements as throwing a softball. Execute the overhand pass from the set position. Your feet should be shoulder-width apart, with the foot opposite your throwing arm slightly in front. Drop your top shoulder toward the ground and cock your wrist back so the pocket of your stick is angled toward the sky. The stick head should be about six inches above your shoulder and six inches behind your head. Pull the stick head up off your shoulder slightly and away from your body. Shift your lower arm slightly forward, but keep the stick on a diagonal. Tighten your bottom hand grip. The grip of your upper hand must be much looser for increased power. Let your top hand slide about a third of the way down the stick before making the throw. This increases the speed and accuracy of the pass.

Twist your torso toward your stick. Consider this a windup. Your upper body provides momentum when you release the ball. Point your lower arm shoulder at the intended target. Step forward with the foot opposite the side your crosse is on. As you step, pull the butt end of the stick down with your bottom hand and snap your top wrist forward. Pull the bottom hand in toward your belly button.

The top hand provides accuracy and direction when passing. The bottom hand provides leverage (strength and power). Think of your lower

Overhand pass/shoulder pass

arm as an actual lever that propels the ball forward. The amount of leverage determines the distance of your pass. The harder you pull down, the farther the ball will go upon release. Your wrists should snap to propel the ball with speed and power. "The biggest thing in passing is to get players to use both hands when they throw. So many players use 80 percent top hand and 20 percent bottom hand. It really is a push and a pull, a snap with the top hand and a pull with the bottom arm," says Coach Wescott.

Follow-Through—Overhand Pass

The most important part of the follow-through is to point the head of your stick at the intended target after releasing the ball. If the ball is released when the head of the stick is at your shoulders, it will be a shoulder level pass. If it is released down by your waist, the pass will be low or bounce along the ground.

Your torso is also an integral part of the follow-through. Twist your upper body with your crosse as you pull it to a side to throw. As you move your arms forward to throw the ball, twist your upper body in the direction of the throw. Your upper body twist provides momentum to send the ball strong and hard.

Always step with the foot opposite of the side where your crosse is. When you complete the throw, the stick should be in front of your body, roughly parallel to the ground, with the pocket pointed at your target.

Work on releasing the ball at the correct time. If you let the ball leave your stick too late, after it passes your head, the ball will hit the ground in front of your target. Conversely, if you release the ball too soon, when the stick is still behind your head, the ball will fly too high and be difficult for your teammate to catch.

Passing to the Right or Left

To pass to a side, pull the crosse back to the top hand side of your body. As you pull back, or wind up, for the throw, step forward with the foot on the side. Twist your upper body to the same side that you pull your crosse back to (your top hand side). Take the next step forward with your opposite foot and throw the ball (if throwing from the right side of your body, step forward with your left foot). Lead with your upper body and twist your torso so your shoulders are square to the intended target. Square means that your shoulders are centered on the person you are passing to. Twist your torso through the throw and end with your top arm shoulder pointing toward the intended target.

Sidearm Pass

The sidearm pass is a great passing style to use when trying to get around an opponent or pass the ball underneath an opponent's crosse. From the set position, drop your top arm out to the side so the stick head is almost horizontal to the ground. Drop your top shoulder toward the ground and twist your torso to this side of your body. Point your top elbow out behind you as you pull your stick head out.

Grip the butt end of the stick tightly with your bottom hand. Your other hand should grip the stick about halfway down. If this hand is too high, you won't have as much control. Lead with your bottom arm shoulder and begin the throwing movement. Step forward with the foot that's opposite to the crosse. Point your bottom elbow at the target, and pull with your bottom arm through the elbow. Twist your upper body forward in the direction of the throw. Push with your top arm as you twist your upper body through to the target. The momentum of your body provides speed for the ball. Flick your wrists toward the target as you release the ball to ensure the ball is passed accurately.

The strength of this pass is the speed and power of the throw. It can be a great shot or a great pass around a defender. However, equally important is the fact that pulling your stick out to the side of your body leaves the stick vulnerable to a check from an opponent in front or behind you. A

Sidearm pass

back check, where the defender is behind you, is legal if your stick head is out to the side. Be sure that no one is coming in from behind before executing a sidearm pass.

Flip Pass

The flip pass is a similar move to the sidearm pass. From the set position, pull your stick head back beyond your top shoulder and down in a semi-circle motion toward the ground. Continue the circular motion until your

Flip pass

wrist is under the stick and the pocket is facing up toward the sky. Step forward with your opposite foot and snap your top wrist up to release the ball. This is a gentle, underhand pass that is used in tight spaces. If your teammate is too close for a strong throw, try this softer pass.

Pop Pass

The pop pass is a great pass to use in the eight-meter arc because this pass involves no backswing. In an area where the defense is tight around you, it is good to know how to pass the ball to a teammate without the big backswing, which is a telltale sign that you are about to release the ball.

From the set position, bring the stick in front of your face. Slide your grip slightly so your top hand is behind the stick, ready to push it forward. Slide your top hand down the shaft of the stick to increase the leverage—and therefore the speed—of the pass.

The momentum for this shot comes from the bottom hand acting as a lever on the shaft of the stick, as well as the top hand pushing the stick head forward. Quickly and sharply pull the bottom of the stick down and in toward your body. As you do this, push forward with your top hand, moving the stick head forward. Snap your top wrist forward when you release the ball.

Pop pass

Underarm/Shovel Pass

The underarm pass, or shovel pass, is great to use when you are tightly marked. The shovel pass is thrown from the bottom hand side of your body. Pull the cradle all the way across your body to the bottom hand side of your body in the full cradle swing (see chapter 3).

Pull the stick across your body to your bottom hand side, and point your bottom elbow away from your body. Twist your body to the bottom hand side and point your top hand shoulder at the intended target. Continue moving your bottom hand back behind your body.

With the top hand, move the stick head in a semicircle motion away from the body and out to your bottom hand side. Move your top and bottom arms in sync, so the crosse makes a circular sweeping motion. With your top hand, pull the stick down and through your waist like you are shoveling snow. The pocket of the stick is facing up toward the sky, and your top wrist is under the stick.

Step forward with your top hand side foot. Snap your wrist up and underhand pass the ball through your waist. After you release the ball, point the stick head at the intended target.

The top hand controls the direction of the throw. As you execute this motion, push slightly with your top hand. Throw the ball out of the stick by giving an extra push with your arms at the end of your shovel motion.

Follow-Through—Underarm Pass

The follow-through of your stick controls the height of the pass. The higher you lift your stick upon release, the higher the ball goes. Conversely, the more level and closer to the ground you keep your stick when you release the ball, the closer to the ground the ball travels.

BACK PASS

You must always feel comfortable moving the ball both forward and backward down the field. There will come a time when you cannot go forward any more because you have either run out of room, or perhaps because the defense won't let you advance. When this happens, turn around and look for a back pass behind you. Passing back opens up the field. If you are stuck, the player behind you may be your only outlet. And chances are, she sees something you don't, or is in a better position to move the ball toward goal.

Follow through

Reverse Pass

From the set position, move your crosse in a full cradle swing over to your bottom hand side. Adjust your fingers to over-exaggerate the rotation of your stick head. Continue bringing the pocket around so it is on your bottom hand side and facing away from your body. This requires extra

Reverse pass

movement from your top wrist and fingers. Lift the stick up and off your bottom hand shoulder.

The set up for this move is similar to the overhand pass, however everything is reversed. Cock your wrist back and angle the stick head up toward the sky. Step forward with your top hand foot and snap your top wrist forward while you simultaneously pull your bottom hand down and in toward your mid-section. Just as in the overhand pass, the top hand directs the throw and the bottom hand provides strength in the leverage. Upon release, point your stick head at your intended target.

Lob Pass

This pass is difficult to master but can be invaluable in certain situations. As the name implies, you lob or toss the ball high in the air to your teammate. The high trajectory means opponents can't block the pass. Ideally, your teammate should catch the pass over her shoulder while on the run. An effective lob pass can advance the ball down the field in a hurry. It can be used to start an offensive fast break following a turnover.

The key is being able to throw the ball ahead of your teammate so she doesn't have to turn around to catch the ball. If she stops, defenders can easily catch up and block or intercept the pass.

The technique for throwing a lob pass is similar to a regular overhand pass. But because the ball must travel farther, take a longer backswing and make a few short stutter steps forward as you throw to create momentum. Your top hand should be about halfway down the stick. Release the ball almost directly over your head to ensure a high pass.

CREATIVE PASSING

Passes can be made from any release point. Wherever you have your stick in the cradling motion, you can always snap your wrist, pull your bottom hand down and toss the ball to a teammate. You can throw the ball behind your back, around your head or over your shoulder. Be creative and have fun when passing. Always experiment when passing with a partner, that's the best time to learn!

RECEIVING

"Catching is crucial. If you don't catch the ball, you can't do anything with it," says Coach Wescott.

The lacrosse stick is an extension of your body. Receiving a pass in lacrosse is much like catching a ball in any other sport. Imagine playing softball, for example. When the ball comes your way, you reach out your glove for it and place your glove in the line of the ball. Remember that when you catch a softball, your hand and glove give slightly to absorb the speed of the ball. The same theory holds true in lacrosse.

Positioning

Before receiving a pass, you must be prepared and in correct positioning. Stand with your feet shoulder-width apart and your knees slightly bent. This is a good athletic stance that allows you to move forward or backward, left or right, to catch the pass. You must learn to receive a pass from different heights and angles. Hold your stick up and out in front of you slightly to the side of your body with the open side of the pocket facing forward. Extend your top arm out so the pocket of the stick is up and out in front of you, bringing the stick head up and out with it. The stick head is now at a 45-degree angle to the ground and above your head. Your top arm is fully extended, but not stiff. Your stick is still on a diagonal, with your lower arm in front of your top side hip. Remember, your arms are going to give with the ball when you receive it, so your elbows must be slightly flexed in preparation for this give.

Let your teammate know that you are ready to receive a pass by calling for the ball. Call for the ball by holding your stick out as described above. This gives your teammate a target and lets her know that you are ready to receive the ball. Move toward the ball as it nears you. If you stand flatfooted, waiting for the ball to arrive, defenders have a chance to close in and bat it away. When the ball gets closer to the stick pocket, resist the temptation to reach out and bat at the ball. Instead, keep the pocket near the side of your head and the stick close to your body. When you receive the ball, keep your eye on the ball from the second it leaves your teammate's crosse until it reaches your stick. As the ball settles into the pocket, "give" with the throw instead of keeping your arm rigid. This will keep the ball from popping out. Once you have control of the ball, rotate your shoulders toward your stick to protect the ball from a defender. Now you're ready to quickly run with the ball, make a pass, or take a shot. Never catch a pass and simply stand in place. Keep moving. Beginning lacrosse players should practice catching balls that are gently tossed to them. This way, they'll learn to carefully watch the ball into the pocket. Always try to catch the ball in the center of the pocket, so it doesn't hit the hard frame and bounce to the ground. Remember to keep your stick high and close to your side as you prepare for a catch. Beginners tend to let the stick fall near their waist, and they lose valuable time raising the stick into position to make a catch.

Top arm catch

Top Arm Catch

Extend your stick toward the ball, on the line it is traveling in, and watch it all the way into your crosse. As the ball enters your crosse, give with the pass and cock your top wrist back. This changes the angle of the pocket so it is now facing upward, settling the ball into the stick head. Pull the stick back to the set position. This is a top arm side catch.

Wrap Catch

Hold your stick out in front of you in the proper position to receive a catch. Watch the ball as it enters your crosse. When the ball is in your stick head, give with the pass and immediately use the full cradle swing to wrap the ball around to your bottom hand side. Remember, the full cradle swing is a semi-circular motion in front of your body. Keep your elbows out and push your bottom hand forward once receiving the ball to keep the stick on a diagonal.

Wrap catch

Never let your stick be vertical to the ground or the ball will fall out of the crosse. "So many times on a wrap catch I see a player go across the ball flat instead of wrapping and turning the stick back to their bottom side shoulder. Or they try to catch the ball too flat with the stick straight up and down and there's no place to give. They need to get the head of the stick out to the ball to receive it," says Coach Wescott.

Nonstick Side Catch

You can receive the ball from any direction, as long as your pocket is open and facing toward the pass. The above description of how to catch was for a typical straight on pass. However, in game situations, you will not always be properly positioned to receive the ball straight on. If a defender is on your top hand side, you do not want to receive a pass on that side. That puts the defender in a great position to check the ball out of your stick. This is when a nonstick side catch (also called reverse reception or weak side catch) comes in handy.

A nonstick side catch is executed on the bottom hand side of your body. Pull the crosse all the way across your body to your lower hand side. The open side of the pocket is facing forward and your top wrist is completely flexed inward.

Nonstick side catch (for a left-handed player)

With your crosse on your lower hand side, extend your top arm out farther to that side and up to call for the ball. Move your bottom forearm upward slightly. Tighten your bottom hand grip. Keep your eyes on the ball at all times as it comes to you. Move the crosse so it is in a direct line with the path the ball is traveling. Watch the ball fall into your crosse.

As you receive the ball, give with your arms to absorb the strength of the pass. As you give, the crosse moves back slightly. Pull the crosse down as it moves back, then immediately move into a cradling motion heading toward your top hand side. Incredibly important in reverse receiving is body flexibility. You must have flexibility in your upper body and trunk in order to twist to receive the ball, and then twist back into a cradling motion. When receiving the ball, twist your upper body to the side, toward the crosse. After you catch the ball, twist your body back toward the opposite side, leading the direction of the cradle.

Receiving High

Sometimes the pass will be too high for you to reach. When this happens, slide your top hand down the shaft of the stick to get a greater reaching distance and use a one-handed catch to get the ball. Holding the stick with one hand increases your reach. For a one-handed catch, slide the ball side hand down to the butt of the stick. Reach up to the ball, and once it enters your crosse wrap catch it with one hand. The wrapping motion of rotating your wrist—and the stick head—in toward your body keeps the ball in the crosse and secures possession. Pull the stick down as you wrap and place your second hand on the stick.

GROUND BALLS

Bad passes, interceptions, or loose balls will often send the ball to the ground during the game. When this happens, you must be able to pick it up as you are running and regain possession. This is called a ground ball pick up. Many of the same principles apply to retrieving a ground ball as to catching a pass. Don't wait for the ball to roll toward you, just as you wouldn't stand flatfooted and wait for a pass to arrive. Go out and meet the rolling ball. Keep running as you scoop it up to make sure you gain control of the ball. Always keep both hands on the stick for greater control.

Remember, defenders will likely be closing in as you pick up the ball. Keep your stick close to your body to protect it and immediately look for open areas to run or opportunities to pass. Technique is important in picking up ground balls, but so is hustle. The player who wants the ball more will usually get there first and gain control of it.

Ball moving away from you

Ball Moving Away from You

When you approach a ground ball that is moving away from you, lower your stick to the ground with your hands still in the set cradling position. Bend at the waist and drop your top arm shoulder. Extend your top arm so the stick head is down and out in front of you. Keep your feet moving toward the ball and your knees bent. Drop your lower hand down so the stick becomes level with the ground. Your stick hits the ground about three inches in front of the ball. Push the stick along the ground so your knuckles are actually touching the grass. Push your bottom hand forward to scoop through the ball, all the while running forward, until the ball slides into your crosse. Immediately begin cradling the ball. If a defender is around, cradle away from the defender, keeping the crosse behind your opposite ear to protect the ball.

Because the ball is moving in the same direction you are, this move is executed with speed and confidence. You must catch the ball and overcome its own speed to get it into your crosse.

Ball Moving toward You

When the ball is moving toward you, the mechanics of the move change slightly. Place the stick head near the ground next to your bottom hand foot. The crosse is vertical to the ground and upside down. When the ball hits the crosse, give with the ball. Your two hands and the crosse move

Ball moving toward you

backward as you give to absorb the ball. Immediately begin the cradling motion with your top hand.

To practice this move, have a teammate roll the ball at you. Go slowly at first, and speed up as your confidence builds.

COMMUNICATION

Passing and receiving are both impossible without communication. You are on a field with 11 other players and you must be able to communicate both verbally and nonverbally with each one of them. Always call for the ball when you are in a position to receive it, even when you are just throwing with a partner in the backyard. This gets you in the habit of talking, and once you move onto the field in a game, you will be in good shape. Similarly, the passer calls out the name of the teammate she is passing to before each pass. Coach Wescott gets her team talking any way she can: "Sometimes when they're warming up and jogging, we'll have them sing a song with their mouthguards in, or chant something over and over."

Not all type of communication is oral, however. There are also more subtle forms of communication. Nonverbal cues are extremely important on the field, because they are less identifiable by the opponent. Practice the following forms of nonverbal communication as you work on passing and receiving.

Eye Contact

The most important nonverbal communication skill is eye contact. From the beginning, you were taught to cradle with your head up so you could see the field. If you're passing, you must be able to see where the best pass is. A teammate in an open space is no good to you if you can't see her. However, after seeing her, you must be sure that she is ready to receive your pass. Accomplish this with eye contact. Perhaps you want the receiver to run down the field into an open space. With your eyes, signal that she should start moving, and throw in front of her so she can run on to the ball. Similarly, as a receiver, you want to give your full eye contact attention to the passer. This ensures that she knows you're ready for the ball. In the moment your eyes meet, you'll know the pass is a go. Eye contact is an entire language of its own.

"Call" with Stick

Another nonverbal cue is calling for the ball with your crosse, which is also known as giving a target. As mentioned in receiving, always use your stick head to indicate where you want the ball. Perhaps you want it out in front of you. Point there with your stick head and give your passer a target to throw to. If there is a defender on your right, but you are prepared to catch the ball on your left, place your left hand on top of the stick, moving the crosse to your left side, and call with the stick head. This indicates to the passer that you're aware of your defender, but are still prepared to receive the ball away from that defender.

TIMING

The last component to passing is timing. You and your partner must be in sync with each other. You know how to throw and you know how to receive. You communicate verbally and nonverbally to ensure that you are both ready for the pass that is about to take place. However, if the timing is off, all your work is for nothing. As a passer, you want to throw the ball so the receiver can smoothly move onto the pass. You don't want to wait too long, forcing her to be stuck in a spot waiting for the ball. Conversely, if you intend for her to run onto the ball, your throw must be accurately placed and timed so that the receiver can get to the area where you are passing the ball. This is called a leading pass. All of these aspects are part of timing.

As a receiver, timing is critical in communicating with the attack player. You must call for the ball, make your move toward the passer or into the open space (which way is determined by eye contact and communication), and smoothly collect the ball and continue your movements.

DRILLS AND GAMES

Catch and Step

Players: Two
Equipment: Two crosses and a ball
Distance: Five to 15 yards

Stand facing your teammate with the ball in your crosse. Execute an overhand pass to your teammate, who is five yards away. Your teammate must catch the ball, throw it back to you, and you must also catch the ball. Once you have both caught the ball at this distance, each of you take one step backwards. Continue this until you are 15 yards apart. If you or your partner drop the ball, go back to the five-yard distance.

Circle Pass

Players: Two
Equipment: Two crosses, one ball
Distance: Five-yard circle

Stand five yards away from your teammate. At the count of three, begin running in a counterclockwise circle, following your teammate. The two of you are following the same circular path. You have the ball. Cradle with your right hand on top, to the right of your body. Cradle and pass across the circle to your teammate as you run. Time your pass so it is slightly ahead of your teammate, so she can run onto the ball. Your teammate catches the ball on the run, cradles, and passes it back across the circle to you. Continue this circular motion for three minutes.

After three minutes, switch directions so you are running clockwise in a circle, cradling to the left with your left hand on top. Pass and receive in a similar style for three minutes.

Shuttle Passes

Players: Four or more
Equipment: Sticks and one ball
Distance: 10 yards

Divide your group in half and stand with one half facing the other, 10 yards apart. Each group forms a line behind the first player in their group. Player one has the ball. She cradles and overhand passes to player two, who is in the opposite line 10 yards away. Player two moves onto the ball to receive the pass. After releasing the ball, player one runs to the end of the line opposite of the one she just came from. Player two throws the ball back to the line she just received the pass from, however now it is player three receiving the ball since player one moved to the back of the other line. Player two switches lines now as player three throws the ball across the 10 yards to player four.

Continue this shuttle drill executing overhand passes for 10 minutes. Once every player is comfortable with passing and receiving on the run in the shuttle, switch to a pop pass. Continue for 10 minutes. After the pop passes are complete, move on to a sidearm pass. Continue rotating passing styles until all passes are executed on the move, and all players are catching the ball. Include ground ball pick ups in this shuttle rotation.

Wall Ball

Players: One
Equipment: Stick, ball, and a wall
Distance: Your preference

Wall ball is one of the greatest exercises you can do to increase your passing and receiving skills, as well as your stick skills. Stand up to eight meters away from a wall with your crosse and ball. Throw the ball against the wall and catch it as it comes back to you. When you throw the ball, practice every style in this chapter and the creative ones you've come up with on your own. When you receive the ball, work on top arm catches, wrap catches, and reverse catches.

As you increase your time against the wall, practice throwing the ball and aiming for what would be your teammates chest and head. The ball will come back at you at your chest and head, which mimics a bad pass. By practicing how to receive awkward passes, you will be better prepared when a teammate tosses you a bad one during a game. To maximize the benefits of wall ball, spend 20 minutes a day, three days a week, with the wall.

Three Person Weave

Players: Three
Equipment: Sticks and a ball
Distance: 30 yards

Start on the center line with two other teammates. Stand 10 yards apart so you are all facing the end line. The player in the middle starts with the ball. She moves forward and passes the ball off to the player on her left. After releasing the ball, the center player cuts behind the player she just passed to on the left. The player who received the ball cradles in toward the middle of the field and then passes the ball out to the player on the right. After passing, she cuts behind the player she just passed to. The player who received the ball now cradles in to the center of the field and passes out to the player on the left. Continue this weaving pattern for the entire 30-yard distance.

Three Person Pass

Players: Three
Equipment: Sticks and a ball
Distance: Width of the field

Three players stand across the field, one on the left sideline, one in the center and one on the right sideline. The player on the left starts with the ball. She passes to the player in the middle, who moves toward the pass, then pivots and immediately sends the ball to the player on the other sideline. The third player catches and sends the ball back to the middle player, who catches, pivots and releases the ball in the opposite direction. Continue passing for five minutes. Switch roles so everyone has a chance to be in the middle. Work on moving to the ball, receiving the ball, pivoting and immediately releasing the ball again.

Monkey in the Middle

Players: Three
Equipment: Sticks and ball
Distance: 10 yards

Two players stand facing each other, 10 yards apart. A third player stands in the middle of the two. The two players on the outside throw and catch back and forth with each other, executing different passing styles. The player in the middle works on intercepting the ball and blocking the pass. She goes after any bad passes, and extends her stick—sometimes with a one arm reach—to knock the ball down. Keep the ball moving quickly between the two players. Once the middle player gets the ball, she rotates with one of the end players.

6
Goal Keeping

GOALIES ARE SPECIAL. THEY NEED A GREATER ARRAY OF MENTAL AND physical skills than any other lacrosse player. They play the highest-profile position on the field. When they make a great save, everyone notices. Likewise, when a goalie gives up a goal, everyone notices too.

A goalie, first and foremost, needs mental toughness. Most of the physical skills can be taught. But if a person lacks self-confidence and aggressiveness, she has no business being in goal. Even the best goalies get scored upon—over and over. Great goalies can't get down on themselves and sulk after a goal. They have to immediately regroup mentally and be prepared for the next shot—or they'll give up another goal.

Goalies must be excellent team leaders, both with words and actions. The rest of the team feeds off the goalie's demeanor. If she gives up a goal and still projects confidence, the rest of the team will remain confident too. Goalies can't blame their defensive teammates when they give up a goal. True, a defensive blunder can lead to a goal. The goalie should point out defensive lapses by teammates, but she can't openly berate a teammate. That destroys team unity and undermines respect for the goalie.

Goalies are like quarterbacks in football. They direct their teammates, shouting out instructions as a ball approaches the goal. They can't be shy. Goalies need great vision and concentration. They must see the action as it unfolds, anticipate what will happen next, and get in position to make a save. The goalie's primary responsibility is to stop shots. She can use her stick, glove, arms, legs, or body to prevent a goal. She also must learn to go out and meet the ball, not just stand on her heels and wait for the ball to come to her.

A goalie can't be afraid of the ball. True, it can sting when it hits your body—another reason to develop excellent stick and glove skills to keep the ball away from you. She must make split-second decisions over and over. A goalie must know when to move to the left or right, when to stay in the crease, and when to gamble and leave the crease to get a ball.

Besides making saves, a goalie has to effectively clear shots after a save. In other words, she must be an excellent passer. Sometimes, she needs to make a quick, short toss to a teammate. Other times, the goalie must loft a long, accurate pass that a teammate catches far down the field on the run. Still want to be a goalie?

WHAT IT TAKES
Communication

The goalie is the leader of the defense. Because you are at the farthest point in the field, you have a better view than anyone else out there. You need to share that view with your teammates so they can benefit from what you see. When talking to your teammates, always use direct, supportive language. Call who is open, who needs to be marked, where the ball is, and where you want your defense to be. Drexel University head coach, Anne Marie Vesco, advises her players to do whatever the goalie tells them to. "The goalie's in charge so I say do what your goalie says no matter what, even if you think it's wrong. She's the one facing the shots, so if she wants a double at a certain time, you go to the double."

TRAINING THE GOALIE

If you're a brand new goalie, you may feel intimidated calling out for the defense to move onto attacking players. Coach Wescott suggests having the coach, or an older and more experienced goalie, help out by standing behind the cage and directing traffic from there. "If I'm training a beginner, I'll stand behind the goal cage and tell defenders when to go so the goalie gets a good idea of when to send a player. And when she sees me directing traffic, she starts to learn when and why she might send players," she says.

But goalies, don't just shout out when you need help, congratulate your teammates when you see them doing something outrageously good too. If there's a fast break coming at you, and your recovering defender gets back there and stops ball, call out your encouragement for the job well done by your teammate. "When a defender busts her butt to get back there and steals the ball, praise her for it. This kind of communication helps the defense to bond," says Coach Wescott.

Body Position

Stand with your feet shoulder width apart, with your weight on the balls of your feet and your knees bent. Raise your chest upwards slightly, as if you are sitting on a stool. Keep your body weight over your feet, not ahead of your feet. It is important that you don't lean too far forward. "Too often the goalie leans forward and brings her chest forward too much so her body weight is forward—it's easy to get suckered into taking a fake when you're too far forward," warns Coach Wescott. Keep your body balanced and relaxed in this position. Your arms should be slightly apart from your body and your elbows comfortably bent. Your entire body should be relaxed, not rigid, but fully concentrating on the action in front of you.

Body position

Stepping to the shot

Stick positioning (correct)   Stick positioning (incorrect)

Stick Position

Always use two hands on the stick when defending the goal cage. The open pocket of the stick faces forward and is always square to the shot when saving the ball. Place your top hand just beneath the bridge of the stick head. The V formed by your index finger and thumb is slightly to the back inside of the stick. With your top hand positioned with the V in this way, you can rotate your wrist to move the stick below your waist for low shots. Your grip is loose enough so that you can rotate the stick in your hand to adjust to the angle of the shot. Your bottom hand is around the butt end of the stick. Goalies don't typically switch hands, so always use your dominant hand on top.

Hold your stick with bent arms in the relaxed set position. Your elbows are bent slightly and outside the line of the stick. Keep your stick on a diagonal with the stick head off the top hand side of your face next to your eyes and your bottom hand holding the stick near your midsection. Angle your stick head closer to your body than the butt end of the stick by holding the elbow of your lower arm off your hip slightly.

As the shooter approaches, line the ball up with the inside edge of your stick head. By doing this you have a clear vision of the ball and you know that your body and stick are protecting the goal cage. If the shooter comes in closer, raise your body up slightly so they can't shoot over you. Be careful, especially if you are tall, not to hold your stick in dead space. Sometimes a goalie sets for a shot and the stick is above the top of the goal cage. It's not doing any good up there—if that's where the shot is, it will not be a goal anyway. Make the best use of your stick and be very aware of your space inside the goal cage.

Breaking Down a Block

There is so much that goes into blocking a shot, the best way to handle it all is to break it down into three elements: "There are three things we work with: their eyes (seeing the ball), taking their hands to the ball, and foot skills (stepping with the closest foot to the shot). So they're saving the ball between their hips and shoulders, and if it misses the stick, it hits the body and goes wide," says Coach Wescott.

Consider these three elements to be your three lines of defense against the shot. You need to see the ball, you need to move your stick to it, and you need to move your body behind it. When you do these three things, you are guaranteed to stop the ball. If the ball misses your stick, your body is there to block the shot.

Breaking this down allows you to focus on one element at a time so you can truly understand what is supposed to be happening and how to time your movement when a shot is coming at you. Don't forget, though, that when that shot comes, it's split second timing. Once you understand what each part is doing, put it all together and make it flow like one movement.

Eyes

You need to train your eyes to follow the shot from when it is released to when it enters your stick. "Most goalies see the ball shot, but they don't really follow it and keep it in the sweet spot of their vision," says Coach Wescott. Everywhere the ball goes, your eyes go. If it's headed over your head, your helmet goes up as the ball passes above you. If the ball is out

Eyes

to the left or right side, your helmet turns to one side or the other with the ball. Always keep the ball in line with your nose. "Sometimes I'll take a ball and stand in front of the goalie and have it where my chin is, then I'll bring it to the right, to the left, and all around," says Coach Wescott. As Coach Wescott moves the ball around the goalie's head, the goalie moves her eyes and her head to follow the ball. This gets her comfortable on two fronts: first, she is growing accustomed to having the ball in her face all the time; and secondly, she is learning how to keep her eyes on the ball and follow it wherever it goes. "The eye is a muscle. Like every other muscle you have to train it," says Coach Wescott.

If the attacker is protecting the stick head and you can't see the ball, look for the butt end of the stick and determine where the stick head is from there. "If the shooter's back is to you, watch her shoulders and the butt of the stick and you'll see which way she's opening, and from the butt of the stick you'll know where the stick head is," says Coach Wescott.

Hands

From the ready position, drive your top hand forward when the shot is released. Your hand takes your stick, and eventually your body, directly to the shot. Rotate the stick with your bottom hand so your stick head is open to the ball with the widest surface area facing the shot. Keep your eyes on the ball.

As your top hand moves to the ball, your bottom hand follows, taking the entire stick to the shot, not just the stick head, in order to get underneath the ball. As the ball comes to you, punch forward with your bottom hand. By bringing your top hand out to meet the shot and punching, or pushing sharply, with your bottom hand, you are creating space behind your stick to step into and getting your body behind the save. When you complete the punching motion, your stick head is closer to your body than the butt end of the stick.

A common mistake goalies make is to pull back with their bottom hand instead of push forward. The stick comes back into the hip instead of moving out in front of the goalie. As a result, the goalie ends up stepping backward instead of forward, and her body never gets behind the shot.

Feet

Your eyes are on the ball, and your top hand drives to meet the shot. Your bottom hand is following the top, and all movements are going out toward the ball. Next up: your feet. You need your feet to bring your body behind the stick and behind the shot. "If they just take the head of the stick to the shot, they don't have that second line of defense against shot—the body," says Coach Wescott.

You always want to step toward the shot with the foot closest to the shooter. If the shooter is on your right, step to her with your right foot. If she is on your left, your first step is with your left foot. When you take this step, always point your toes directly at the shooter's stick. You want to be square to the ball. Do not square up to the shooter's body because she may be holding the ball out to one side or the other. The ball isn't coming from her body, it's coming from her stick.

As you step into the shot, step to the post at a 45-degree angle so that if the ball misses your stick and your body, it's definitely going wide off the cage. "When the goalie finishes her step, her hip is in line with the pole of the cage. The shot is either going to hit the stick, hit her body, or go wide," says Coach Wescott. Use your body placement to outwit the shooter. And no matter what, avoid crossing your feet over in front of each other—this knocks you off balance.

Angles

Imagine there is an arc that starts at one post, comes off the goal line about one and a half steps, and ends at the other goal post. Use this imaginary line as a guideline during play. To travel along this arc, take small quick steps referred to as set steps. As the shooter comes into the eight-meter arc, step along the arc to stay square to the shooter. Always move quickly, and keep your feet shoulder width apart. As soon as you step down with your stepping foot, quickly pull your second foot in so your feet are always shoulder width apart.

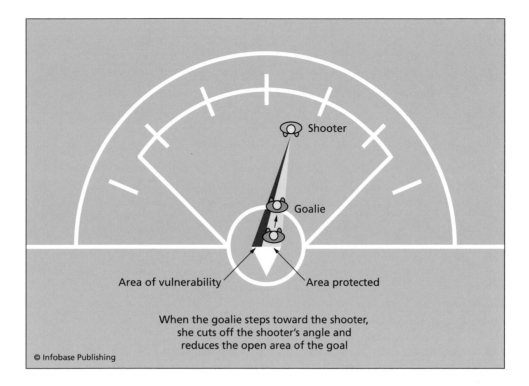

Shooter

Goalie

Area of vulnerability   Area protected

When the goalie steps toward the shooter,
she cuts off the shooter's angle and
reduces the open area of the goal

© Infobase Publishing

In addition to your imaginary arc, create an imaginary line that starts at the back center of your goal and goes straight to the shooter. To reduce the shooter's angle, step out along this line to the point where it intersects with the arc. It essentially makes the goal cage smaller for the shooter.

Typically, you don't want to come out more than two or three steps from the goal line. However, Coach Wescott points out that each goalie is different, "It depends on how tall and how quick the goalie is. If she's a little taller she can be out a little more. If she has quick reflexes she can play out a little more." Any goalie might be comfortable doing something that another goalie can't stand, so play around with whatever you feel most comfortable doing. "Start back and see how quick you are and if you can use your height, come out more. You typically don't want to come out more than two or three steps off the goal line unless you're going out for an interception or ground ball," she says.

Blocking in Action

Now it's time to put the above elements together and make it one fluid movement. There are two kinds of blocks, overhand and underhand. The basic elements do not change, though. Keep your eye on the ball, drive your top hand to the ball, and step into the shot so you are square to the ball. Do not make any move until the ball is released. The most common mistake a goalie makes is coming out to the ball too soon. The shooter may be faking a shot or pumping her body to lead you to one side. If you come out too soon, you will fall for her fakes. You don't know where the shot is going until it comes off the shooter's strings, so be patient.

Overhand Block

The overhand block saves any shot coming in above the bottom of the breast. Keep your eye on the ball and be prepared for a shot as soon as the shooter comes into the eight-meter arc. Put the mechanics of the block together as described above. First come out to the shooter to reduce her angle, keeping your shoulders square to her and staying on your imaginary arc line. Keep your eye on the ball, drive your top hand to the shot, step to the shot and keep your body square to the ball. Punch your bottom hand forward when you receive the ball and end with your stick head closer to your body than the butt end of the stick.

Nonstick Side Overhand Block

The overhand block is used above the bottom of the breast on either side of your body. Your dominant hand always stays on top. When crossing over to your nonstick side, the same mechanics apply as on the stick side block.

Nonstick side overhand block *(above and on following page)*

Underhand Block

If the shot is coming in below the bottom of the breast, you must make an underhand block. Low shots and bounce shots are examples of shots saved underhand. It is critical that you don't move underhand until you are sure the shot is coming in below your breast. "I see some players go underhand too high, so the only thing facing the shot is the tip of the crosse," says Coach Wescott.

In the ready position, the V formed by the index finger and thumb of your top hand is behind the bridge and slightly inside the stick. From this position, you can easily pull your wrist down and out to the top hand side of your body to move the stick head to the shot, without having to alter your wrist position. As you do this, drop your elbow out to keep the pocket moving downward. Keep the open pocket of the stick head square to the ball. Pull up with your bottom hand on the butt end of the stick as you move the stick head down with your top hand, so the stick makes a semicircular motion traveling off the side of your body.

Remember, as you drop the stick drive the top hand to the shot. This requires you to overturn your wrist slightly to create the room to step into the shot. If you don't move the stick head forward, you don't create the room for your body to step to the shot. You need this second line of defense against an incoming shot. "A lot of goalies bring their stick back toward their feet to make a low save and it makes them step back instead of stepping forward and into shot," says Coach Wescott. Remember, always move into the ball—not away from it—when blocking a shot.

If the shot is coming in along the ground, continue pulling your bottom hand up so the shaft of the stick is perpendicular to the ground and above the stick head. Punch forward with your bottom hand on the butt of the stick to stop the ball and step in behind the shot with your feet together for extra protection.

Nonstick Side Underhand Block

If the ball is coming in along the ground on your nonstick side, start with the same movements described above but continue crossing the stick head in front of your feet, so it is on your nonstick side. Pull out and up with your bottom elbow, keeping the elbow pointing out to the side and away from your body. Carry the stick through until it reaches the shot. Drive the top hand underneath the stick head to the shot, step into the shot keeping your body behind your stick, and punch with the bottom hand when you receive the ball.

Nonstick side underhand block

Waist Shots

The most difficult shots to save as a goalie are those shot around your waist, particularly on your nonstick side. Always use an underhand block when making a waist save. "A lot of times goalies aren't in line with the shot when it's at the waist," says Coach Wescott. It's particularly hard because the ball is coming in so close to your body, there's a natural tendency to step away from, not toward the shot. Treat the waist shot as you do any other. Drive the stick head to the ball first. By moving the stick head forward, you create the room for your body to also take that very necessary step forward to get behind the ball.

Stick Side Waist

On the stick side, drop the stick head down and to the side of your body as you do during any underhand block. Keep your top hand just underneath the bridge of the stick head. Pull the stick head out and to the side of your body with the open pocket facing forward.

Since the shot is coming in at your waist, continue pulling the stick head in to your body. Your wrist is cocked back to keep the stick head facing forward, and your top hand side elbow is pointing directly behind your body. Your bottom hand pulls the shaft out to the opposite side, so the stick is parallel to the ground. "You're going to drive the butt of the stick sideways," says Coach Wescott. This angle will change depending on where the shot is heading. Take the top hand to the shot so the open pocket is in front of your stick side waist. Then step behind your stick so your body is behind the shot, also. Punch with the bottom hand to absorb the impact of the shot so the stick head is closer to your body than the butt end.

Nonstick Side Waist

On the nonstick side of your body, pull the underhand block all the way around as if you were saving a ball on your nonstick side. The stick is perpendicular to the ground with the stick head closest to the ground. Your top hand is still just underneath the bridge of the stick head. Now continue pulling the stick through, taking the top hand and stick head up to your nonstick side waist. The stick is still upside down, but the open face of the pocket is forward, facing the shot, in front of your nonstick side waist. Your bottom hand is still around the butt end of the shaft. Your bottom wrist faces forward and is cocked to keep the stick at a perpendicular angle. Once the stick head is in position to meet the shot, step forward into the shot and get your body behind it.

THE MENTAL EDGE

You are in the goal cage every practice and every game. Players are throwing the ball at you day in and day out. You need to have a mental edge to be on top of your game. Coach Wescott suggests adding distractions while you're practicing your blocks and clears. If you hate a certain kind of music, set up a stereo behind the goal and get that music playing. Learn how to stay focused during even the most frustrating times!

It is important, too, to remember that a goal scored is the result of an entire defensive slump. It is never just the goalie's fault or just a certain defender's fault. "It's a defensive unit, and you all got scored on. It's not just the goalie's job to keep that ball out of the goal cage. The defenders also must realize they have a duty to protect the goalie," adds Coast Wescott.

It's important to recognize the difference between a good goal and a bad goal. "If you didn't see the ball, you made a mistake. If you saw the ball, took your stick to it, and stepped to it, it's a good goal. Sometimes time and space are not on your side," says Coach Wescott. When the ball goes in the cage, analyze the situation. "Did you step right, did you see the ball? You can do everything right and guess what, she still scored. It's going to happen," she says.

Bounce Shots

Goalies should try to stop all shots in the air. Balls that bounce in front of you can be the most difficult to stop. Why? Because natural turf is rarely completely smooth and level. As a result, balls can take crazy and unpredictable bounces—and get past you in a split second. When you see a shot headed for the ground, immediately get prepared. Lower your body—not by bending from the waist, but by crouching low, in the same way a baseball catcher does. Lean forward slightly. Take a wide stance and keep your stick well in front of your body. The top of the stick should be angled away from you, with the pocket touching the ground near your feet. Watch the ball intently as it hits the ground and bounces toward you. With a proper stance, you're prepared to block the ball with your stick or your body.

Clearing

Once you block the shot, you need to clear it as far out of the defensive end as you can. To effectively do this, collect the shot that you blocked and control the ball in your crosse.

You always want to clear the ball toward the sides of the field. Never clear up the middle of the field. This is a dangerous area and, if intercepted, the offense is right where you don't want them—in front of the goal. If possible, clear the ball to the opposite side of where the shot came from. "Wherever the ball comes from, look deep to the other side of the field first and work your way back," advises Coach Wescott.

To clear the ball, bring your stick up in front of you and slide your top hand about halfway down the shaft of the stick. Sliding your top hand down gives you greater leverage to send the ball farther down the field. Slide your bottom hand down to the butt end of your stick.

Continue bringing the stick head over your head and behind your top hand shoulder. "A lot of goalies don't bring the stick up before they throw

Clearing

so they're throwing off their shoulder and they wind up pushing the ball. When you throw the ball you don't throw it from your shoulder, you bring it back behind you because you have that protection of the crease," says Coach Wescott.

The clearing movement is much like throwing a softball. Step in opposition with your bottom hand foot forward in the direction of your target. As you step, rotate your hips through so they are square to your target. Move your top arm forward and flick your wrist as you release the ball. Pull with your bottom hand in toward your midsection. Follow through, bringing your stick all the way across your body to your opposite hip and stepping forward with your top hand side foot.

You have ten seconds to clear the ball out of your crease. Depending on the situation, you may choose to send the ball out to an open teammate immediately. You just shut the offense down and they may settle into a lull right after the shot. Use their break down to your advantage and get the ball moving into your offensive end immediately.

Other times, you may choose to hold onto the ball for a few seconds before clearing to allow your defense to organize. You also might hold onto the ball if an attack player is pressuring you and staying right on the edge of your crease. Gather the ball and take a step first to the inside of the crease, away from the attacker. This step gives you protection against that pesky attack player. "Once you make that save, move into a position where the player who is pressuring you can't block your clear," says Coach Wescott. If your right hand is up, step to the left so that the crease protects your stick. If your left hand is up, step right.

If you're still feeling pressure from her, use the goal cage as a pick. Move behind the cage—all the while staying in your crease—and clear the ball from there. Placing the cage between you and the attacker gives you more room to feel confident about your clear.

AVOID BRINGING DOWN THE RAIN

You always want the clear to be a strong line drive. If your clear is looking more like a pop-up, go through the mechanics of your throw slowly to pinpoint the problem. Chances are, you're dipping down when you throw the ball. "A common problem is that goalies bring the stick up and back and then dip down to throw it, and the angle of trajectory winds up being an arc instead of a line drive. Keep the stick on the diagonal plane so you can snap with your top hand and pull with your bottom hand and make the path of the ball straight instead of having that huge arc that will bring rain down from the clouds," says Coach Wescott.

Behind the Net

When the ball is behind the goal, you must turn around so that you can see it. The feeder is usually more toward one side of the goal than the other. Always turn toward the side that the ball is on. Keep two hands on your stick and stay in a set position. Always stay in front of the goal, so you are facing the open net.

There are two ways to face the ball when it is behind the goal. The first is to stay in the center of the goal. "Split the cage with your navel and turn so your shoulders are square to the ball," says Coach Wescott. If the feeder changes positions and moves the ball, adjust your shoulders so you are always square to the ball.

The second approach to facing the ball behind the goal is to move ball side slightly. If you're facing the goal and the ball is on the left side, line your outside foot up with the outside pole closest to the ball. If you are quick at intercepting passes coming from the feeder, this might be the better position for you because it moves you closer to the ball. However, it also takes you slightly off angle from the center of the goal, so be prepared to adjust when the ball comes around to the front side of the cage.

One-on-Ones

Often times, a goalie is called upon to stop the ball herself. Perhaps your defense didn't get back in time. Maybe the attack player broke through the defense and is right in your face. Or perhaps you went out for a loose ball thinking you'd beat the attacking player, but she got there first. You can't turn and run from her now, you've got to defend her and stop her shot from going into the cage.

As a goalie, you have your choice of whether or not you want to step out to the shooter, or stay back on the goal line until the shooter releases the ball. "Whether a goalie steps out and blocks the shot depends on how quick and how tall she is. It's a personal thing. Some goalies sit back and wait to smother the shot, and some go out to cut off the angle," says Coach Wescott.

Whichever approach you take, the most important thing when you come one on one with an attacker is to line your stick up with hers. If her stick is far out to the right of her body, don't pay attention to her body but focus on getting in the set position directly in line with her stick.

Once you're lined up with her stick, wait for her to shoot the ball. Once she releases it, drive your stick head to it and step toward the shot to get your body behind the ball. Be prepared to take your stick straight up to stop a high shot, or out to the side to block a sidearm shot if the attacker attempts to send a shot around you.

Rolling the Crease Block

Another form of one-on-one occurs when the feeder behind the cage rolls the crease and comes around to the front side in an attempt to slip the ball into the net. Remember, when she is behind the goal, you are in front of the goal facing the feeder. When you see her start to come around the inside of the crease, step to the post that she is moving closest to. Always step with the foot closest to the post. If you're facing the goal and she starts moving in on the side of the left post (when you are facing the cage), take one quick step with your right foot directly to the post. Plant that foot next to the post and quickly bring your left foot in next to your right. Your legs, hips, and upper body line up directly next to the post so nothing can get between you and that post. Hold that position.

Do not come off the post until the shooter moves into the eight-meter arc. "Most goalies leave the post too soon when the shooter's on the 12-meter line, and they give the close post up. Wait until she is inside the eight meter area," advises Coach Wescott. As she moves, stay on the post but turn your body so your shoulders are always square to her. Once she enters the eight-meter arc, step off the post toward the shooter, keeping your shoulders square to her and your toes pointing at her.

If she continues to follow the crease toward the center of the goal, step toward the center of the crease, centering your body in the middle of the goal and keeping your shoulders square to the shooter. At this point, don't move toward her any more, just protect the crease and keep your body in the center of the goal and your shoulders and stick square to hers.

ADVICE FOR GOALIES AND COACHES

If you're ducking from the ball every time someone takes a shot, it's time to rethink your position. "Some goalies are afraid of the ball, and that's not a good thing. If you duck out of the way, it's a problem," says Coach Vesco. If you turn your head and close your eyes when the ball comes at you, it's a problem not just for your team, but also more importantly for you.

"It's hard to find, but the goalie is the kid who isn't afraid of the ball, who wants to take on the challenge of getting in the cage and making the saves," says Coach Wescott. The worst thing to do is stay in the goal if you're fighting with the ball everyday. "You're not going to be good and you're not going to enjoy it," she adds.

As a coach, recognize when it's time to search for a new goalie. Pull a few players aside and throw tennis balls at them.

See who goes for the ball, and who shies away from it. The player who steps forward to catch the ball could be your new goalie. And your old goalie could be your new standout field player.

Interception

Another talent a goalie must possess is the ability to intercept the ball. This can happen at various times, often when the feeder is behind the goal and sends a pass over the goal. Feeders have a tendency to forget about the goalie. It is the perfect time for the defense to gain possession.

The ball is behind the cage and you are centered in front of the cage with your shoulders square to the goal. If you are prepared to intercept, move toward the side of the goal where the ball is. Line up your outside foot with the post of the goal, as discussed above. Do not swing your stick around to show off your reach. Often times goalies think they are intimidating the feeder by showing their reach. In reality, what this is doing is showing the feeder exactly where not to pass the ball. Keep it a surprise. When the feeder releases the ball over your head, extend your stick up and back. Your stick head is actually over your head and back slightly, angled toward the sky. "When you go to intercept, you either want to go straight up or back behind your head a little bit. Use your bottom hand to throw the stick toward the ball so you can reach as high as you can," says Coach Wescott.

Another opportunity to intercept the ball is if attackers are passing in front of the crease. Be poised and ready to go for the ball. The trick is that you never move to the ball unless you are 100 percent sure your will get the interception.

Outside the Crease

At some point or another, you must come out of your goal to go for the ball. This could happen when a shot goes wide, or it could be that you blocked a shot that rebounded out of the crease. You might be the closest player to the ball, and must therefore get there first to gain possession. Once you decide to leave the crease, don't second-guess yourself. If you hesitate and wonder if you made the right choice, the offense can score a quick goal. Get to the ball quickly, before defenders can close in on you. With experience, you'll be able to judge distances and determine when to leave the crease and when to stay put. When you approach a ground ball, you must pick it up quickly and cleanly.

Move toward the ball and drop your stick head down to the ground so it is actually grazing the grass. Drop your back arm and hand down toward the ground so the entire stick moves just above the ground, with your stick head touching the grass. Bend at your knees and your waist and get low to the ground. Keep your eye on the ball and watch it move into your crosse.

Once the ball is in your crosse, bring your top hand up to the side of your head, and look for a teammate to pass to. You must be able to throw accurately under pressure. Remember, you cannot re-enter the crease with the ball once you have left the crease.

Equipment

Goalies wear more equipment than any other player. You need the proper equipment, and it must fit correctly. You shouldn't feel weighed down by your equipment. Instead, it should give you confidence to play aggressively and not fear being injured. Here are the basic items you need: helmet, chest protector, gloves, thigh pads, shin pads, throat guard, and mouth guard. Each item comes in a variety of sizes and styles. Ask your coach or an experienced player for guidance on which to select. Of course, besides the protective equipment, you need a goalie's stick.

They are distinctly different than ones used by other players. In short, they are bigger and heavier—specifically designed to stop shots. Stick styles vary widely. The handles are usually made of titanium, aluminum, or alloy—lighter materials than wood. They come in a variety of lengths. The mesh pockets can be hard or soft. Try out several sticks, if possible. Find one you can handle well, that doesn't seem too big and bulky. When you like your stick, your confidence soars.

DRILLS AND GAMES
Shuffle Steps

Players: Goalie
Equipment: Goalie equipment and cage
Distance: Goalie crease

Start at the right post of the goal cage with your stick in your hand. Shuffle step across the goal line until you reach the left post. Count how many steps it takes to get there. Shuffle back to the right post and count those steps. Shuffle to the center of the goal and tap the top of the cage with the top of your crosse. Keep your stick head open and facing forward. Sprint forward to the top of the crease, then drop step with your left foot back to the left post, lining your body up tightly with the post. Shuffle again to the middle of the goal line and tap the top of the cage with the top of your crosse. Sprint to the top of the crease and drop step back to the right post, lining your body up with the post so no shot could get in between you and the post.

Count how many steps it takes to get from one spot to the next. This trains your mind to understand how far your body has to travel without having to look at the posts.

Eye Ball/Hand Ball

Players: Two
Equipment: Helmet, small colored rubber balls, gloves, one wall
Distance: five feet

Stand five feet in front of a wall, facing it; wear your helmet. Have your teammate or coach stand behind you, also facing the wall, with a variety of colored rubber balls. The teammate throws a ball at the wall over your head. As soon as you see the ball, call out the color and then step to it and catch it. Dot not move for the ball until you shout out the color first. Then take your hands directly to the ball and step with your body behind your hands and the ball. Catch the ball and roll it back to your teammate behind you. As soon as you roll the ball back, your teammate sends the next one in over your head. Once you are comfortable doing this, put a stick in your hand. Call the color and move to the ball with your stick, driving first with your top hand. Remember to break down your steps into three sections: eyes, hands, feet.

Colors in the Cage

Players: Two
Equipment: Goalie equipment, goal cage, sticks, small colored rubber balls
Distance: Eight-meter arc

Stand in the goal cage in all your equipment and your stick, with your back to the top of the eight-meter arc. Your teammate or coach is at the top of the eight-meter with a pile of colored balls. When your teammate yells shot, turn around and face her in the set position. As soon as she yells, she throws a ball in at the goal. You yell the color of the ball, and then make the save. Do not make the save until you call out the color of the ball. Drive your top hand to the ball and step forward with your close side foot.

Your teammate moves around the eight-meter arc so that you don't always know where the shot is coming from. Practice a variety of shots.

COACH'S TIPS

Often times, a coach will increase the size of the crease for a beginner at the start of the season to get her used to playing in that area. In reality, this is a disservice to the goalie. The goalie becomes accustomed to working in a large area than is allotted, and come game time she'll feel pressured in the smaller crease.

It's also a good idea to create competition in practices. Divide the team into offensive and defensive sections, and have them compete during practice for points. At the end of the practice, the winners get to sit out on a sprint. Better yet, make the non-winning team do an extra sprint! "If you never create competition in your practices, they're not going to be used to it in a game," says Coach Wescott.

A Game of Throw and Catch

Players: Two
Equipment: Goalie equipment, sticks, and ball
Distance: 10 yards

Stand 10 yards away from a teammate. Start with the ball and clear it to your teammate. Work on the mechanics of the clear. She catches the ball and sends it back to you. This is simple enough, but it is important that you warm up just as everyone else on the team does. Practicing your throws allows you to practice your clears. The more you practice, the more accurate your clears are, and the more you can take part in the offensive transition out of your defensive end.

Shots on Goal

Players: Three or more
Equipment: Goal cage, goalie equipment, sticks, and ball
Distance: Eight-meter arc

Two players start on either side of the end corners of the eight-meter arc. They each have the ball. The goalie is in the cage. The player on the right shoots first, and the goalie blocks and clears the ball out to the other player on the opposite side of the arc. That player then receives the ball and shoots it back at the goalie. The goalie blocks and clears it back to player one, who has moved up the arc slightly more toward the center of the arc. This continues until both players meet and take shots from the top of the eight-meter arc.

Faking It

Players: Two
Equipment: Goalie equipment, goal cage, stick, and ball
Distance: Eight-meter arc

Start in the goal cage facing the top of the eight-meter arc. Your teammate is at the top of the eight-meter with the ball. The teammate sometimes fakes a shot and sometimes takes a shot. You must yell out when you think she is taking the shot. She is going to try to get you to yell "shot" when she is faking it. Be patient and wait for the shot. Remember, you're not making your move to block it until you yell shot when it is released from the shooting strings.

Interceptions

Players: Three
Equipment: Goalie equipment, goal cage, sticks, and ball
Distance: Eight-meter arc

Start in the goal cage facing your two teammates. One teammate is on the edge of the crease to your right. The other is at the top of the eight-meter arc. The two teammates simply throw the ball back and forth to each other. When you feel ready, step out and intercept the ball. Don't go until you are confident that you can get the ball. The two teammates throwing the ball are not making it hard for you to intercept, they are simply throwing and catching near you. This drill is to get you comfortable with the idea of stepping out of the crease for the ball.

Once you are comfortable intercepting at this distance, the player on the edge of the cease takes one step farther away from you. The two continue throwing and catching the ball. When you feel comfortable, step out and intercept the ball. Every 10 catches, after you've completed at least one interception, the player near the crease takes another step away from the crease. You continue to try to intercept the ball, always starting on your goal line in the crease. This drill will get you accustomed to how far you feel comfortable coming out of the crease and it will give you a better understanding of how far your reach is.

Shooting on the Run

Players: Five
Equipment: Goalie equipment, goal cage, stick, ball
Distance: 12-meter fan

Form three lines, two on either side of the eight-meter arc and one behind the goal. You are in the goal. The first line, to the right of the goal, starts with the ball and runs into the arc, comes face to face with you and attempts to place a shot around you. You are working on your one-on-one skills. If the ball goes in, the next line goes. It you make the save, clear the ball out wide to the left, the opposite side, and prepare for the next line to go. The second line comes from behind the goal. The player rolls the crease and tries to slide a shot in. The play ends when the ball goes in the goal or when you clear it out far to the side. Then the third lines goes, with the player on the left moving onto you. These shooters try a variety of shots, attempting to place the ball in all corners of the cage.

Rebounds

Players: Five
Equipment: Balls, goal equipment, goal cage, sticks
Distance: 12-meter fan

Form two lines on either side of the eight-meter arc. One player stands behind the goal with a pile of balls. The player at the head of the left line starts with a ball and moves onto the goal, taking a shot. If the ball goes in, the player behind the goal rolls a ball out from behind the cage as if it was a rebound. The attacker and goalie fight for the rebound. If the goalie gets it, she clears wide. If the attacker gets it, she shoots again. If the goalie blocks the ball and there is no rebound, she clears it wide and the next player goes. If there is a rebound, the attacker and goalie fight for possession over the lose ball. Once the ball is cleared, the next player from the opposite line moves onto the goalie and the drill is repeated.

7
Shooting

In lacrosse, nothing beats the thrill of scoring a goal. Games are often high scoring, so it's important to be able to match your opponent goal for goal. Unlike soccer, lacrosse games rarely end with only a few goals on the scoreboard.

Shooting is a distinct skill, just like passing and receiving. It's much more complex than it may appear. You don't simply hurl the ball at the net and hope it gets past the goaltender.

Remember, lacrosse is one of the fastest sports. Players are constantly on the move, so don't expect to shoot from a standing position with no one around you. You'll probably have to dodge around several defenders to have an open shot. You may have only a split second to get off a shot, so be prepared to fire it. No one likes a player who shoots every time she gets the ball. Passing and teamwork are essential. But when you have a good chance to score, don't opt to pass instead.

Once you decide to shoot, you must aim the shot properly. You don't want to shoot the ball *at* the goalie. You want to shoot it where the goalie can't reach it. Normally, you want to fake to the left or right, even slightly, to try to move the goalie one way or the other. That creates a greater opening. Often, the best places to shoot are in the upper and lower corners of the net. Those are areas the goalie has the most difficulty reaching. Also, it's generally best to shoot on the goalie's nonstick side. That way, she has to bring her stick across her body to make a save, increasing the difficulty.

In shooting, speed and placement are the two keys. As you get farther from the net, the velocity of the shot becomes more important. On a slow shot, the goalie has plenty of time to get in position for a save. When you're close to the goal, placement is much more important, since the ball doesn't have to travel far.

There are many different types of shots, and you should try to master them all. We'll discuss each below. The fundamentals are generally the same. Your top hand should be about halfway down the stick, your bottom hand near the end. In tight spaces, you can bring your hands even closer together for greater control.

In every shot, you want a quick release. This gives the goalie less time to react. Work on snapping your wrists as you shoot the ball. This increases the velocity. Shooting doesn't involve strength. Instead, it's about form and execution. The smallest player on the field can be the best shooter.

THE BASICS

Practice

As with anything else in lacrosse, the key to being a good shooter is practice. "Shooting is all about practicing over and over—repetition. Basically, the first step is to start working on your stick work. How you feel the ball in the stick is really important and that all comes from doing lots and lots of stick work," says Coach Vesco. This chapter discusses a variety of shots, but above all it enforces creativity in what you do on the field. Take time to understand the mechanics of these shots, and then get on the field and let it flow. Creativity is important. Work on releasing the ball from different positions. Be unpredictable and keep the goalie off balance. During every team practice, work on your shooting skills. But you can also practice alone. Shoot the ball against a tall concrete wall. Work on your placement and accuracy. Envision game situations. The best shooters are those who practice over and over.

Balance

One important element of shooting is keeping your body balanced. Your body must always be ready to twist, dodge, dart, and shoot. Keep your feet moving, keep your head facing toward goal, keep your crosse protected, and keep the goal in your mind's eye.

You need to maintain a level of control over your body as you move toward the goal and take a shot. Part of it comes from increasing your flexibility, and part of it comes from keeping your weight on the balls of your feet and keeping your knees bent—even as you dodge—to maintain a low center of gravity.

Visualize

Goal scoring is a mental thing. Before you step on the field, you need to be in the frame of mind that you are going to be successful. If you feel intimidated before you even get out there, you're never going to get the ball into the net. It's all about attitude and knowing that it can be done. And one way to get there is visualization.

Visualization borders on meditation. But relax, it's not as corny as it sounds. It's a legitimate, successful form of mental practice.

To perfect your moves, take time each day to mentally practice what you are physically trying to do. Picture yourself moving down the field, around the back of the net, wrapping your crosse around the cage and slipping the ball past the goalie. Picture yourself cutting in front of the goal, receiving a pass from a teammate who's behind the net and immediately sending the ball into the corner of the cage. Every night before bed, take time to visualize the fluidity of these movements. See the ball coming into your crosse and then into the goal. See the goalie's head turn as the ball moves past her body. Visualize every detail, and soon you won't be asking yourself "*Am* I going to score this game?" but rather "*How many* goals am I going to score this game?"

Patience

You have to take chances in front of the goal. The more shots you take, the more likely you are to score. But use your power wisely. You also have to know *when* to shoot. "If you're cradling fiercely, then you shouldn't be shooting—it's just not a good opportunity. Also avoid taking the big cradle before you shoot so you're not telegraphing when you're going to shoot," says Springfield College's coach Emily Kiablick.

There is so much movement in front of the goal because the offense is cutting around and the defense must move to keep up. Every time the ball moves around in front of the goal, the goalie repositions to check her angles. As a shooter, be aware of these transition moments. If you see the goalie take her eyes off you and check her angle in the cage, shoot the ball!

THE SHOOTING LANE AND DANGEROUS SHOTS

Before taking any shot, it is critical that you first check that there is a clear shooting lane. It is up to the defender to get out of your shooting space, or she will get called for a shooting space foul. If you see a defender in your line to goal, pump fake a shot to draw the foul on her. If you shoot the ball into a defender who is in your pathway to the goal, it is a dangerous shot, which is a major foul.

TYPES OF SHOTS

"A good shooter has great stick work and normally has a variety of different shots she can use—not only overhand," says Coach Vesco. There are many different types of shots, and it is important to understand the mechanics of each one and to practice all shots with both hands. You must feel comfortable shooting the ball with either hand up. You must also feel comfortable shooting the ball from any spot near the goal—from behind the net, from the sides of the eight-meter arc, as well as the top of the eight-meter arc. If you only focus on one shot, you limit your options and restrict your flow during the game.

Take time now to practice a variety of shots while you are learning the entire game. The payoff comes later when you have an arsenal of shots that you can execute from any spot in front of (or coming from behind) the goal.

STEP IN OPPOSITION

Step in opposition refers to the practice of stepping with the foot opposite of your top throwing hand. The idea is that when taking a shot, or passing the ball, as you move into the shot you

(continues)

(continued)

step forward with the foot opposite from your top hand. When you step in opposition, you are putting your body weight behind the ball and providing more momentum in your shot. Completely follow through by bringing the stick across your body, and complete the shot or pass by stepping forward with your top hand side foot.

Overhand Shot

The overhand shot is just like the overhand pass, except it is stronger and harder. It uses the same body movements as throwing a softball. It is a strong shot and good to use if you are taking a shot from far range.

Drop your shoulder down and cock your wrist so the open stick head is angled toward the sky. Raise your stick up and bring your bottom arm up and forward slightly. Keep the stick on a diagonal across the front of your body.

Aim with your lower arm shoulder by pointing it at your intended target. Twist your torso toward your stick and away from the goal to really get your body behind the ball. Step in opposition toward the goal and pull the butt end of the stick in toward your middle. Twist your torso toward

Overhand shot

the goal with your shot. As you do this, push forward with your top hand. Flick your top wrist forward to release the ball strongly.

Unlike the overarm pass, when shooting the ball continue your follow through all the way across your body. "When you're throwing, you're stopping your follow through a lot higher. When you're shooting, the ball might release sooner, but you're following through all the way to the ground," says Coach Kiablick. This provides extra speed and momentum.

During any shot, you've got to keep your body weight behind the shot. As you move the crosse forward to execute the shot, keep your shoulder behind your stick head. In doing this you transfer your body weight into the ball as you shoot. This helps with the strength and velocity of the shot. "Throw" the crosse forward and across your body, twisting your torso with the shot. Once your stick passes your midsection, step forward with your top hand foot. When you finish, the stick head is pointing diagonally down toward the ground on the opposite side you started from.

Bounce Shot

The bounce shot is a hard shot for the goalie to block because she has to react to both where the ball is released and where it hits the ground. Typically, the goalie only has to concentrate on where it is released. The bounce adds an extra element for the goalie to consider.

Bounce shot *(above and on following page)*

The bounce shot is a good one to take if you are farther out from the goal and you have a clear shooting lane. It is also a good shot to use when you are approaching the goal with plenty of room. It is a strong shot because you have momentum on your side as you move in toward the goal.

Imagine you are in the set position in front of the goal. Protect your crosse so your bottom hand shoulder is pointing toward the goal. Keep your top arm shoulder back away from the goal with your stick head in the set position. Step in opposition with your bottom hand foot with your toes pointing at the goal. As you step, push forward and down with your top hand and pull your bottom hand, and the butt end of the stick, in toward your middle. Pulling down strongly with your bottom hand provides the necessary leverage to get a strong shot off. Keep your top elbow pointing away from your body. Flick your wrists forward to release the ball.

The farther away from the goal the bounce occurs, the higher the ball goes. If you want the ball to travel high over the goalie's shoulders, aim for a spot outside the crease. If you want a small bounce, aim for a spot just next to the goalie's feet. Practice all types of shots to understand how the ball responds to the ground at different speeds and release points.

Shovel Shot

The shovel shot is good to use when you are tightly marked in the eight-meter arc. It is the same movement as the shovel pass, but this time you're passing it into the goal. Recently, some coaches have shied away from teaching this as a shot. As a result goalies don't have much practice defending against it. As a shooter, the element of surprise is your best friend, so this is a good shot to keep in your back pocket.

Pull the crosse to the bottom hand side of your body and point your bottom hand elbow away from your body. Twist your torso with your stick and point your top hand shoulder at the intended target. Continue moving your bottom hand back behind your body. Move the stick head in a circular motion away from your body and toward your bottom hand side. Pull the stick down and through your waist in a similar motion as shoveling snow. Keep the pocket of the stick facing toward the sky and your top wrist underneath the shaft of the stick.

Your top hand provides the aim during this shot. When you release the ball, push with your top hand and throw the ball out of the stick head.

Sidearm Shot

The sidearm shot is another strong shot that can be used from a distance. However, another excellent time to use the sidearm shot is if a defender is in front of you. Using the sidearm, you can cleanly send the ball around the defender. Coach Vesco agrees: "A good shot when you have a good defender on you is to slide your stick to the side and shoot around your defense."

From the set position, drop the stick head out to the side of your body. Drop your forearm down so your elbow is at a right angle and your forearm is parallel to the ground. This is a quick and easy transition from the set position.

Grip the stick tightly with your bottom hand and slide your top hand about halfway down the shaft of the stick. Moving your top hand down provides more leverage in your shot and will send the ball farther and harder. It also gives you a greater reach around your opponent.

Twist your torso back toward your stick and pull your elbow back slightly to gain momentum. Then push forward with your top hand, keeping the stick parallel to the ground, and pull the butt end of the stick in toward your mid section. Flick your top hand wrist to release the ball. The release point is out to the side, away from your body and away from any defender that is positioned directly in front of you.

> ### PROTECTING THE CROSSE
>
> When you are going in for a shot on goal, it is critical that you always protect the crosse. This means that you use your body as protection between the defense, the goalie, and your stick. When you are facing a defender or the goalie, your bottom hand shoulder and bottom hand foot are the closest parts of your body to the goal. Your torso is facing sideways, and your shoulders are in a line moving away from the goal. Your top hand shoulder is farthest from the goal, and your stick head is in the set position on top of your top hand shoulder. In this way, your body provides protection against the defense and makes it difficult for them to check you.

Pop Shot

The pop shot is great to use when you are tightly marked in the offensive area. If you're in the eight-meter arc, this shot is perfect because it requires no back swing, which eliminates the possibility of being checked from behind. Coach Vesco is a big fan of the pop shot.

"An example of when to use the pop shot is when you dodge around your defender and you now have her on your back. You can do a pop shot, which has no back swing so you can seal the defender off from checking you from behind. And there's no follow through with your stick. It's not a hard shot but a placed shot," she says.

Bring your stick up so it is perpendicular to the ground with the pocket just above your top hand shoulder or in front of your face. In this position, you completely seal your defender off from getting you from behind. Move your top hand down the shaft of the stick slightly so that it is behind the stick and in a position to push the shaft forward. Your top hand provides accuracy for this shot. As your top hand pushes the stick forward, pull the bottom of the stick down toward your body quickly and sharply with your bottom hand. The bottom hand acts as a lever, propelling the ball forward. As you release the ball, snap your top wrist forward.

It is important to concentrate on the benefits of this shot. It is not a strong shot, but a quick move that places the ball in the net.

"The trick is to be able to use the pop shot from different release points. The advanced player can use a pop shot from the right side with her left hand up, or vice versa, or from the middle of her face. It doesn't have to be hard, just tight and placed around the goalie," says Coach

Vesco. She suggests that you become comfortable with releasing the ball from different spots around your head and off your shoulders.

Quick Stick Shot

The quick stick shot is a close relative of the pop shot. The only difference is that it is a fast catch and release shot. As the name suggests, with the quick stick shot, you do not have possession for long.

Cut in front of the goal and call for the ball by giving a target with your stick head. The feeder sends you the ball. This shot works best if the ball is received directly in front of the goal. After receiving the ball, immediately release the shot. There is no back swing and you do not have much speed, but you are popping the shot to a certain spot in the goal. The advantage to this shot is the speed at which it is executed, not necessarily the speed at which the ball travels. Before the goalie can even comprehend that you have received a pass, your shot is already moving past her head into the goal.

You need to be prepared to release the ball before you've even caught it. Think about where you want it to end in the net. However, don't jump the gun. Feel the ball in your crosse and give back slightly before you release it. Often times players run into trouble when they attempt to shoot the ball before fully controlling the catch. Some coaches advise players to internally say a word to themselves before shooting the ball. "Careful," "catch," or "shot," are some common words players use.

Rolling the Crease

If you are the feeder (the first or second home) you need to be able to roll the crease from behind the goal and slip a shot in past the goalie. This trick requires quick stick work and quick moves.

From behind the goal, when you begin to make your move around the crease, your defender will move with you. To effectively roll the crease, you've got to cut to the inside of your defender so you're face to face with the goalie. Imagine you're moving around the right side of the goal, coming from behind. Head toward the side of the net and pump fake to the right, stepping quickly onto your right foot away from the crease. Your defender will shift to stay in front of you. When she does, pull back and come in close to the crease, moving around the circle and sealing your defender off (keeping her on your back side). If her stick is blocking your path, duck under her stick and continue moving onto the crease. You are now rolling the crease. Keep your crosse close to your body and protect it with your shoulders as you roll.

Typically, in this situation the goalie comes out to meet you, so you need to get a shot off quickly. A pop shot is good because the defender you just sealed off cannot check you from behind. If you have the room and the goalie is coming out to you, a sidearm is also a good shot to use to shoot the ball around the goalie. Figure out what you feel most comfortable doing, and then practice a number of other options so that you can guarantee a goal when you roll the crease.

> ### PLACING A SHOT
>
> Placing a shot refers to the concept of literally placing the ball into the net. The idea is to pass the ball to a spot in the goal (obviously, to one that is not where the goalie is standing). Placing a shot works best when the goalie is moving or looking away. Often times, the goalie will have to check her angles, which means she will look down to see where she is in relation to the posts and the goal. When she does this, you can place a "pass" just beyond her top shoulder, for example. Speed is not as important as accuracy when it comes to placing a shot.

Moving the Goalie

A common offensive strategy is to move the goalie before shooting. This can mean a variety of things, however the concept stays the same. In moving the goalie, your motion draws the goalie out of position. "If the goalie is on the midline, you want to move her to one side or the other," says Coach Kiablick. Once you move her toward one side of the goal, place a shot in the opposite side of the cage.

If you are running across the goal left to right, for example, the goalie will move with you out toward your right. You can then place the ball back into the top left corner. "In order to place your shot when you're on the move in front of the cage, you have to feel where the ball is in your stick and get it to a sweet spot right underneath the shooting strings," says Coach Vesco. Once you feel the ball in that sweet spot, you can direct it to any place in the goal you choose.

If you are coming in low with your knees bent and your shoulder dropped so the stick is down low, shoot the ball up high and place it in a top corner. If you are coming in up high, drop low underneath the goalie and place it in the bottom corners or at the goalie's waist level. Cut in front of the cage and ask for the ball up high, and then drop down and shoot it low through your knees. Changing the release spot is critical when you

Placing a shot in the top nonstick side corner of the cage

have the goalie on the move. You are compounding the factors she has to react to, and every time you do that, you have an advantage.

Whichever way you choose to move the goalie, you must always remember to stay balanced and focused in your shot. Because you are running in one direction and shooting in another, you must twist your torso. This requires great flexibility. Keep your trunk flexible and loose when moving the goalie, and be prepared to move in any direction depending on where you see an open space in the net.

SHOOTING HOT SPOTS

There are certain spots that are more difficult for the goalie to block. Always aim for the corners when you are shooting. A top corner on the goalie's nonstick side is a great spot to shoot for. She uses her stick to save, so if you move it to a corner far away from her top hand side, you're more likely to get that goal. Bottom corners are just as effective too.

Another great spot to aim for is the nonstick side waist of the goalie. This is a tough spot because it's hard for the goalie to get her stick head there. "A hard shot for goalies is anything that is hip height. Goalies are trying to save with their sticks, and that's really awkward for them," says Coach Kiablick.

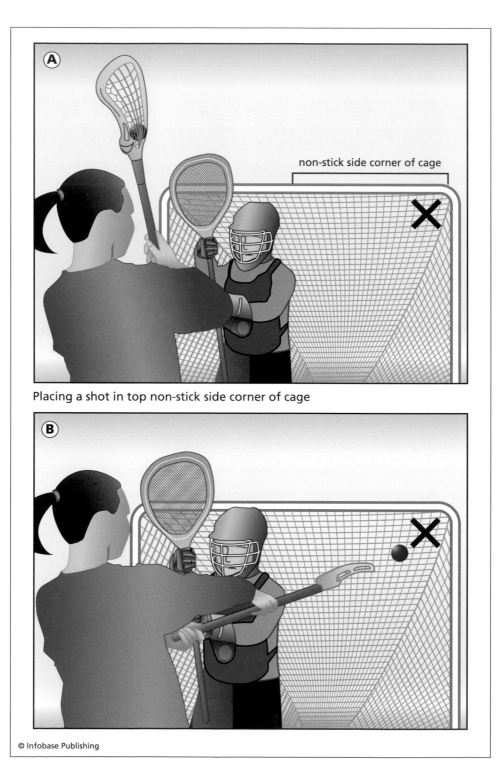

Placing a shot in top non-stick side corner of cage

Soft High Shot

The soft high shot is similar to the idea of moving the goalie. This shot is great to take when you're close to the crease and when you release the ball directly in front of the net. Start in the set position and just before you're about to shoot, lift your crosse high above your head with your top hand over your head. From here, you can shoot the ball in any direction. The higher the crosse, the more difficult it is for the goalie to anticipate and follow.

FAKES

Whenever you're going in for a shot, throw a body fake or a stick fake to confuse the goalie. If you move your head and shoulders in one direction, you'll have the goalie moving in the cage to cover that spot. Then you can easily place a shot opposite of where she is. It doesn't take much to throw a goalie off her angles.

You can also use a variety of stick fakes to get the goalie moving in the wrong direction. Gently throw your stick forward in a shooting motion, but before releasing the ball rotate the stick head around with your top hand. Twist your top hand wrist and fingers in toward your body. This moves the pocket around in a semicircle so the opening faces you. In doing this, you stop the ball from ever leaving your crosse. The goalie is on the move to block your fake shot. As she falls for the fake, pull your crosse back and shoot the ball to a spot in the goal far from where the goalkeeper is heading.

Eight-Meter Shot

The eight-meter shot is also called a free position. When the defense commits a major foul within the eight-meter arc, the attack player who was fouled gets the ball on the eight-meter line and the fouling defender is stationed four meters behind the attack player. The attack may pass, run or shoot the ball as she pleases. Most times, attack players in this situation run and shoot the ball.

Coach Kiablick advises that if you are going to run the ball in for a close shot, your first step should always be away from the defender, even if that means you're moving toward your weak side. Although it may be a natural impulse to run straight toward the goal to try to get the best shooting angle, if you first move away from the defender you give yourself more space for any shot. Then you can move into goal and release whatever shot works best for you, depending on what angle you have.

The second option of shooting the ball from the eight-meter spot is sometimes not taken advantage of because beginners might feel that their shots aren't strong enough to make it to goal. "A lot of girls don't have that kind of power until the higher levels," says Coach Kiablick.

But Coach Kiablick has a solution for this too—it's called the crow hop. "If you're taking the eight meter and you're looking for a powerful shot and not a placement shot, a lot of coaches teach what is called a crow hop," she says. The crow hop is a series of steps that help to get your body weight behind the ball and therefore execute a strong, solid shot. Get in position to shoot with your bottom hand shoulder closest to the goal. Your body is facing sideways toward the sidelines of the field.

When the ref blows the whistle for the shot, step toward the goal with your bottom hand foot, but keep your upper body facing sideways. Take a second step toward the goal with your top hand foot, stepping behind your bottom side foot when you go. Your third step is taken with your bottom hand foot again. As you take this third step, swivel your hips so they are square to, or facing, the goal. Step down with your bottom hand foot with your toes pointing toward the goal. As you move through this third step, begin your overhand shot, or bounce shot, or whichever shot you have chosen to take. Remember to keep your body weight behind the ball and follow through with your crosse all the way in front of your body.

This crow hop movement is smooth and fluid. The faster you move in the steps, the faster your shot gets taken, and the more speed you have in the shot. This is a great trick for beginners who need the extra speed in a far range shot.

Reverse Shot

Use a reverse shot when you're moving across the goal and you want to change your stick head position to the other side of your body. With a reverse shot, you can do that without changing hands.

Imagine your right hand is up, but you want to release the ball from the left side of your body. Bring your stick over, keeping your right hand on top, and cross your right arm over your chest so your stick head is off your left shoulder. Shoot the ball from this position as you would an overhand shot. Rotate the stick head so it faces the goal. Step toward the goal and snap your top wrist forward to release the ball. With your bottom hand, pull the shaft of the stick down and toward your middle, rolling the ball off your shooting strings.

> ## SWITCH HANDS AND SHOOT
>
> Another shot to use in a similar situation is to switch hands first before shooting. Imagine you're moving into the goal with your right hand up, protecting your crosse. Your defender is in front of you toward the right, in line with your crosse. The goalie is also following the ball and is lined up with your stick. A simple way to throw off the goalie and your defender, and to gain extra room, is to switch hands first to get your left hand up and your stick off the left side of your body. Then send off a shot quickly before the goalie changes her angles.

Rebounds

Sometimes the goalie blocks the shot, but doesn't control the ball and the ball deflects off the goalie and out onto the ground in front of the crease. This is called a rebound. When the goalie gets behind the ball, or if a shot dings off the bars of the cage, the ball bounces back into play in the critical scoring area. At this time, you need to push, flick, scoop, slide, or do anything you can to get the ball and send it back into the net. One of the most important things to remember about shooting is to follow your shot and pay attention to the rebounds. When the ball rebounds out, it can either be an opportunity for the defense to gain possession and transfer to offense, or it can be an opportunity for the offense to score. Always make it a scoring opportunity. You're facing the goal, you can see what happens and where the ball is going. Get there and get the ball into the net.

EXPERIMENTAL SHOTS

As you develop your shooting skills, start to experiment with some more advanced shots. Below is a good shot to practice, however remember, creativity reigns above all else in lacrosse, so feel free to experiment with all kinds of shooting styles.

Around the Head

This shot is best used when you're in close to the goal. It is a gentle, skilled shot not a strong, forceful one. It's also a crowd pleaser, so you're sure to be a hit when you use this one!

Around the back

Imagine you're in front of the goal with your stick in the set position, moving toward the net. Protect your crosse and keep your weight on the balls of your feet and your knees bent.

Pull your stick head back and behind your head so your top hand elbow points out and away from your body. Slide your top hand slightly down the shaft of the stick to give you greater reach in getting the crosse around the back of your head. Lift your elbow and shoulder up and move the stick head behind your head and out the opposite side, with the pocket facing the net. With your top wrist, flick the stick head forward so the ball projects out of the stick and into the net. As you flick your top wrist, pull down with your bottom hand to give the ball speed as it leaves your stick. This shot can also be done around the back. Simply lower the stick head as you move it behind.

To execute this move in all its glory, you need momentum in your stick. It is important that you feel the ball in the strings of your crosse and that you are confident that you will be able to send it out strong. Surprise is the key element of this shot, however you also need to make sure the ball leaves your crosse! Practice the mechanics slowly at first, and then try it out faster and faster until you have a fun and unique shot that will catch the goalie off guard.

It's All About You

Everyone can learn the same shots, but it's up to you make a shot perfect. Coach Vesco suggests that each player comes up with a trademark move. This is a move that always works to get you open. Your trademark move is the one that never lets you down, and the one that you can do in your sleep.

The next step is to practice a shot that accompanies that move, and practice it to perfection. Come game time, when the pressure is on, and your team needs a goal, you pull out your trademark move, get your shot off and score the game-winning goal!

Finesse and Creativity

Style is as important as anything else. Lacrosse is an amazing, free-flowing, graceful sport. Take this and run with it. In this book, at camps, at training programs, you will learn certain fundamental shots that every player should know. But please don't think that when you master these, you are done. This is just the beginning, and these certain fundamentals are just the building blocks to your success. Understand them, practice them, and then build on them. Become creative in your style. "When you're shooting, you've got to be able to move your stick around so you can get the ball around the goalie—don't just come from the same spot on your shoulder every time. Have a variety of different shots all over each side of your head," says Coach Vesco.

Have fun out there. Envision an inspiring shot that would make the goalie stop and say, "What just happened?" and then break it down in your mind. Step by step, practice that type of unbelievable shot, let it become part of your body and your movements. And one day when you're moving in on the goal, your finely trained body will explode to make an unbelievable shot and the creative juices will flow. Develop your finesse, be creative, and have fun. Now you are playing lacrosse.

DRILLS AND GAMES

Rebounds Rule

Players: Two
Equipment: Sticks, ball, goal
Distance: Crease

Start with one feeder behind the net with a pile of balls. One attack player is in front of the goal at the top of the eight-meter arc. The feeder rolls the ball through the crease from behind the net. This move simulates a goalie deflecting a shot and creating a rebound. The attack player runs onto the ball and either scoops it up and immediately releases a shot, or simply pushes it back into the net. The idea is to get offensive players thinking about rebounds, and prepared to react to them when they occur in games.

As players become more advanced, add a goalie into this drill. The goalie also moves onto the ball in an attempt to clear it out of the crease and defensive area. This element adds pressure onto the offense and makes her think more on her feet.

Quick Sticks

Players: Three and goalie
Equipment: Sticks, balls, goal, two cones
Distance: Eight-meter arc

Place one cone on either side of the eight-meter arc opposite the goal. One player stands at each cone. The third player is behind the goal with a pile of balls. The goalkeeper is in the net. At the same time, both players cut diagonally in front of the cage so they are passing by each other, calling for the ball by giving a stick head target. The feeder passes to either of the two players. The player who receives the ball quickly releases it with a quick stick shot into a top corner of the cage. Both players stay for the rebound. The drill is over when the ball is in the net or when the goalie passes it out to the top of the eight-meter arc to one of the top two starting lines.

Run and Pop

Players: One or more
Equipment: Stick, ball, goal, four cones
Distance: 12-meter fan

Set up four cones in a direct line in front of the cage. The first cone is at the top of the 12-meter fan. The second cone is one yard in front of the first, heading toward the goal. The third is one yard in front of the second, and the fourth one yard in front of the third. Start at the first cone and weave in and out of the line of cones, dodging at each cone. Practice a different dodge at each cone. Once you move past the fourth cone, close in on the goal and pop a shot into a top corner. Aim specifically for the corners. Once you shoot the ball, return to the end of the line at the top of the 12-meter fan. To increase the difficulty in this drill, add a goalie into the mix.

Six Shooter

Players: One
Equipment: Stick, six balls, goal
Distance: Eight-meter arc

Start at the top of the eight-meter arc next to a pile of six ball. Set your stopwatch and begin by scooping the ball off the ground and quickly shooting it onto goal Quickly scoop and release until all six balls are gone. Stay on your toes and keep your knees bent and your body balanced as you shoot. When you are done, stop the stopwatch and see how long it took you to shoot all six balls. Then count how many went into the net. Each time you do the drill, aim to increase the amount of goals scored, and decrease the amount of time it takes to complete the shots.

Move your pile of balls to another spot on the eight-meter arc and time yourself again. Keep moving around the arc to practice shooting at different angles.

Top Corners

Players: One
Equipment: Sticks and ball, masking tape, goal
Distance: Eight meter

With a piece of masking tape, create a triangle in the top two corners of the goal. Start on the top cross bar about six inches from the corner, and secure a piece of tape there. Stretch the tape on a diagonal down to the side post. Secure that tape to the post. The result is a triangle in the top corner of the goal. Do the same on the other side. Start on the eight-meter arc and practice shooting the ball so it goes into the top corners. Run in from the 12-meter fan and get right up to the crease, and then place the ball into the corners. Continue shooting for one minute nonstop. When time is up, count how many goals you scored from which areas of the field. Notice where your weak areas are and concentrate your shots in those areas to improve your shooting.

Four Corners

Players: Four
Equipment: Sticks and ball, goal, four cones
Distance: Eight-meter arc

Create a square with four cones using the top of the eight-meter as the top of the square. The four cones are about five yards away from each other. The square is directly in front of the goal. Pass the ball around the square, in any direction including diagonals, four times and then shoot. Whoever has the ball after the fourth pass takes the shot. When it is time for the shot, everyone in the square yells "SHOT." When it is your turn to shoot, don't take a long time setting up the shot, but rather quickly release the ball in any kind of shooting style. Make this drill as game-like as possible by passing intensely and accurately. Don't let any balls get away from you. Do this for five minutes.

8

Team Offense

LACROSSE IS A TEAM SPORT. NEVER FORGET THAT. IT'S ESSENTIAL THAT you learn individual skills, such as passing, dodging, catching, and shooting. But a team comprised of star players won't win many games unless they working together as a unit.

Players must be aware of what their teammates are doing at all times. Coaches dislike players who get the ball and then dart off on their own, oblivious to their teammates and the opportunities they might have. If you're not cognizant of others, you could miss a chance to make a pass that could lead to a score. Once your teammates realize you're not a selfish player, they're more likely to get you the ball when you could score. So everyone benefits when girls play as a unit.

THE BASICS

Teamwork

One of the most important aspects of the offensive unit is working together as a team. "You need to make sure everyone is on the same page," says Coach Vesco. There are 12 players on the field, seven of whom will be in the offensive end together at one time or another. If you don't all work together, the end result is nothing less than chaos. A big part of teamwork is believing in your teammates. You've got to trust that every player out there is doing the best job that she can. Expect nothing less from your teammates, and nothing less from yourself.

Positions

Regardless of what position you start in, you may be required to play offense at any time. If you have the ball and are moving into the offensive attack zone, don't stop running because you're a point and you don't think you should be that far up the field. The major attack positions are described in detail below, however even defenders can learn a thing or two in this chapter. It is so important to be a balanced player and understand the inner-workings of the attack unit so that you not only understand what your teammates are doing, but also so you can fill in for anyone at any particular time when needed. (And the same will be expected of the attack players when we get to the team defense chapter.)

First Home

The first home is normally the first line of attack. She is good at moving in and out of small spaces, receiving the ball while being tightly marked, and shooting quickly and accurately. Typically, the first home is the feeder behind the net, sending passes to cutting teammates for scoring opportunities.

The first home has excellent stick work and dodging skills. She also must remember that she always has to retrieve shots taken by teammates that go wide away from the cage. First home cannot crowd the area in front of the goal. As a player who is on the attack in that area of the field, she must always be aware of how many players are in front of the net and how many defenders are nearby.

Second Home

The second home is often referred to as the playmaker. She connects between offense and defense, passes the ball, and shoots. The second home is always cutting and looking for open spaces in front of the net. Second home works closely with first home, and sometimes feeds the ball from behind the cage. Her moves are essential to a strong offensive strategy. She has excellent stick work and dodging skills, and is an excellent shooter with the ability to execute a variety of shots.

Third Home

The third home is a connector. She is used frequently in the transition from defense to offense and is able to distribute passes to attack wings and first and second homes. The third home must be a very smart player. She is always aware of maintaining a balanced attack. If an attack wing moves to another role on the field, the third home switches to the now vacant role and balances out the attack. The third home also must be ready to cut down the center of the field for shots and passes at any time. As a home, this player receives the ball in tight areas and uses her stick work to get accurate shots off.

Attack Wings

Attack wings connect the offense to the defense. As an attack wing, you rule the midfield and unite the team as one unit moving down the field. Attack wings are always alert to spread the game out and change fields. If the play is stuck on the left side of the field, you have to be aware of this and know that when you get the ball, it's time to change things up and move the ball to the right. Attack wings have good endurance and speed to move up and down the field quickly.

Because there are two of you on the field, you have to work together. If one attack wing has the ball and moves in toward goal, the other wing moves in closer to the goal to be a passing option.

Center

The center position is the "connector" on the field. Like the attack wings, the center has to be constantly moving up and down the field to keep the attack and the defense units of the team in sync and ready for transition from one end to the other. She is the most athletic player on the team, and is capable of completing anything and everything that is asked of her. Her primary offensive role lies in the fact that she starts with the ball at the center draw. It is up to her to direct the ball to her teammates or to herself so that her team gains possession and is on the offensive attack from the first seconds of play. The center is also a key player in the defensive unit.

Offensive Strategy

When your team transitions to offense, you are in one of two positions: either you are the ball carrier, or you aren't. These two divisions are referred to as on-ball movement and off-ball movement. Both are equally important to a strong offensive unit. If you are the ball carrier, you need to play smart, yet aggressive to make things happen. If you are off-ball, you need to be constantly on the move to get open for a pass or to create space for the ball carrier. This is critical. There is no offensive unit if off-ball players are just standing around watching the ball carrier.

Challenging the Goal

As the ball carrier, the first thing you need to know going into the attack is to challenge the goal and challenge hard. When you challenge the goal you drive forward into the goal area in an effort to score. When you do this, one of three things will happen. The first is that no one will pick you up and it's a one-on-one situation with you and the goalie. In that case, there's no excuse—you know a number of shots that you can execute in a number of different situations, so score!

In the second scenario, a defender picks you up. This is your perfect opportunity to use one of your well-practiced dodges and get around that defender. Another option here is to pass to an open teammate. Always know when to pass and when to dodge. Typically, you can read your defender to determine whether you will be able to dodge around her. If she's crowding your space and you can't get a move off, take a step back and pass the ball.

The third scenario is that you are double-teamed. This might sound frightening and make you feel as if you have failed in your efforts. But that is not the case. Consider the double team a compliment to your attacking skills. They're afraid of you, and one girl can't handle the job. Every time you draw the double team, it gives one of your teammates the opportunity to be open, so look up to find the open player. When you find her, make eye contact. Step back and away from the double team and send the ball to your open teammate, or sidearm pass around the double-teaming defenders.

In each one of these three scenarios, challenging the goal results in action in front of the goal. As the attacking unit, your team's ball carrier has got to make the first move to stir things up.

Offensive players should remember to use the space behind the goal. Most fields extend 20 yards behind the net. That's a lot of room to maneuver with the ball.

Smart players will position themselves behind the net and look for open teammates in front. A quick, accurate pass from behind the net often results in a goal. Goalies have a hard time following a pass from behind the net. They must turn around to see the ball.

If the offensive player makes a quick pass, it's difficult for the goalie to turn back around and get in a good defensive position to stop the shot in front of her. Never lob a pass to a teammate in front of the net. A soft pass allows the goalie time to readjust and defenders time to knock down the ball or intercept it. Passes from behind the net must be quick and on the mark.

Wherever you are on the field, be creative and unpredictable. Don't make it obvious where you're headed with the ball. Don't telegraph your passes. Strategy is key in lacrosse. You must be able to fake out the defenders to get in a position to score.

Look for opportunities to capitalize upon. For instance, you may notice that one defender seems particularly tired. You may be able to easily maneuver past her and get in a position to pass or shoot. Also, you may spot a player who isn't as talented or experienced as you are. Again, you have a chance to gain an advantage by challenging her.

On the other hand, don't be intimidated by a player who seems superior to you. Proper strategy, movements, and fakes can triumph over sheer talent.

> ### A COMMON MISTAKE
>
> Coach Vesco points out that a common mistake players make is that they don't spread out enough in the offensive end. Often times, players—especially beginners—get too caught up in being close to the ball and to the goal. The result is that all the attacking players are clumped next to each other. "A lot of times people stand next to the ball and just watch, and that's no good because you're not creating lanes. And your defense is just standing there waiting," says Coach Vesco. The solution: spread out!

Off-Ball Movement

Consequently, if you are off-ball, you're constantly moving around to create lanes for the ball carrier and to keep the defense moving and confused. You may cut to an open space and look for a pass. Or you may vacate an area and allow a teammate who has the ball to move into the area. See diagrams below. The attacking team is only good if it's a team in motion. If you don't have the ball, it's just as critical that you are in motion—even more so—than if you do have the ball. No one is ever standing around watching the play. The play itself is dependent on the moves of the entire offensive unit.

As this chapter continues, the cutting section will outline certain moves you can do as an off-ball player to effectively create space and to move the defense.

CUTTING

The best way to start off a game is by cutting around your defender. Right from the start, let her know that you're not going to make her job easy. The basis of cutting is to quickly and sharply move away from your defender in an attempt to get into an open space and receive a pass, or to create an open space for the ball carrier. All defenders know this will happen at some point during the game, but if you start off cutting, you'll have your defender sweating and distraught after the first five minutes of play.

Most offensive cuts occur directly in front of the goal. It is in this area that you need to be on your toes to cut in and receive a pass from the feeder. Or, conversely, cut out and bring your defender with you so you create space for the ball carrier entering this critical scoring area.

One tip to remember when cutting is that you always want to move into an open area. No teammate is going to pass you the ball if you've just moved yourself—and your defender—into an area where there are already too many people.

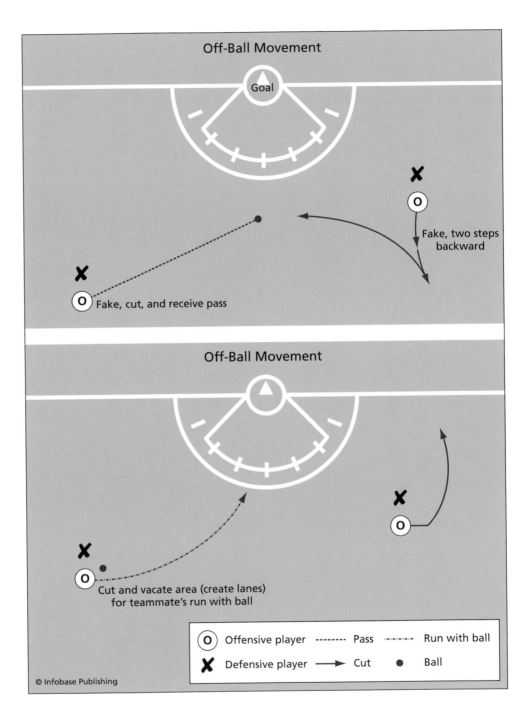

Off-Ball Movement

Goal

Fake, two steps backward

Fake, cut, and receive pass

Off-Ball Movement

Cut and vacate area (create lanes)
for teammate's run with ball

O Offensive player	------- Pass	-·-·-·- Run with ball
X Defensive player	→ Cut	● Ball

Cutting to Receive a Pass

When cutting away from the defender to receive a pass, the first step is to draw your defender out of the area you plan on cutting into, creating space for your cut. Imagine you're in front of the goal and marked by a defender. Your feeder is behind the net. You need to move out of that area and take your defender with you so you can quickly cut back in to receive a pass in front of the goal. When doing this, you must keep your eyes on your defender. "You've got to pull the defender out with you, so make sure you're looking at her," says Coach Vesco. With your eyes on the defender, back pedal out of the area in front of the goal.

Once you pull her out of the area, continue to stay focused on your defender. As soon as she takes her eyes off you to look at the ball, make your move. One of the important things to remember about offense is to play off what the defender is doing. Always keep your eye on her and know where she is, if she's paying attention to you or not. Determine your next move based on her.

When you make your move, explode off your back foot and take off in the direction of your cut, lifting your knees high as you go. Always stay on the balls of your feet and take small, quick steps. This keeps your body weight balanced and allows you to change your direction, if necessary.

Always cut into a space where you can receive and play the ball. Undoubtedly, your defender will follow you. However, the first step you gain on her can make or break your cut. It's amazing what a little extra time can do. If you move into the center of the goal area and for just one second are unguarded, that means you're free to receive a pass and quickly send a shot into the net . . . GOAL!

THE FEEDER

"The feeder is confident in stick skills, is very strong, and spends a lot of time in the eight-meter arc with high pressure. She needs to fake passes and make passes," says Coach Kiablick.

The feeder is the player (usually behind the goal) with the ball who passes to you when you are cutting. As a feeder, always protect your stick and the ball from the oncoming defense. Remember, when protecting your crosse, keep your lower hand shoulder toward the defender, your body turned sideways away from her and your stick head off your top hand shoulder. When you are ready to pass, move toward the player you are passing to. Another option you have as a feeder is to throw a fake to confuse your defender, and then pass around her.

If you are positioned behind the goal as a feeder, make sure to stand on one side of the net or the other. Do not stand directly behind the goal. Too often, feeders forget about the goalie and send a pass directly over her head, which the goalie can easily intercept. "A good feeder needs to be aware of everything going on around her and not forget about the goalie—goalies pick off passes too," says Coach Kiablick.

When passing the ball, pass flat, fast, and accurate. Look for players who are cutting into open spaces and read where they want the ball. Pass directly to the stick head. As a feeder, you must practice your passes so they are always on target. You don't want a bad pass to result in a turnover. If the defense is going to get the ball from you, at least make them work for it.

Body Language

Anytime you are cutting, you need to be certain you're the only one making that particular cut. Nonverbal communication with your teammates is critical here. "Look up and make sure you're not cutting at the same time as a teammate," says Coach Vesco. There are many types of nonverbal communication skills you can develop to interpret a teammate's body language.

First of all, whenever you are about to cut, you must make eye contact with the feeder. Let her know that you are ready to receive a pass. In addition, always give a target with your stick head. This means that as you make your cut, you hold your stick out in front of you with the pocket facing the feeder. "When you cut through, you need to go full speed, and you need to look like you're going to get the ball, so give the target," says Coach Vesco.

This is a clear sign that you are ready for the pass, and it is also the perfect way to show the feeder exactly where you want the ball. Other nonverbal cues include head nods in a certain direction where you are going, or where you want a teammate to cut. The most common cues used, however, are eye contact and stick head targets.

Cutting to Create Lanes

Another reason for cutting is to pull your defender out of a crowded area to create space for the ball carrier. Unlike the above cut, in this move you are taking yourself and your defender out of play. This can be done for a number of reasons. Perhaps a teammate is heading into the eight-meter arc and she needs a clear shooting lane. Or, perhaps it is just too crowded in the eight-meter arc and everyone is just getting in each other's way. Have faith that your teammates will get the job done and pull out.

When creating lanes for the ball carrier, make your move on the ball carrier's top hand side. If you clear out the area on that side of your teammate, she'll have more room to protect her crosse and move around her defender.

When you cut away from the goal, you need to make your defender think that you are going somewhere with a purpose. All cuts, no matter what, must be defined, distinct, and fast. Give a stick head target as you cut out. Your defender will think you are going for a pass, and will be sure to move with you.

If you are slowly walking away from play, or if you're checking your nails instead of watching the ball, your defender is going to know you have no intentions of getting involved in the play. She can leave you and move in to a double team situation against one of your teammates. You don't want that to happen. Make eye contact with the defender when you are pulling out. Sprint around the outside of the crease, behind the cage and to the other side of the field. Make your defender think you're executing a play. And don't stop—slow down to a jog, then speed up again and take her for a ride.

CUTTING TIPS

- Always use short, quick passes. This gives the defense less opportunity to intercept.
- Cut on sharp angles.
- If you cut and do not receive the ball or create a space, keep moving out of the area and reposition yourself for another cut in for the ball. Never give up if you cut and don't get anything— keep moving and keep working for a pass.

Backdoor Cut

A common cut is the backdoor cut. In this move, you cut around your defender and slide in behind her toward the cage. "Backdoor" means you have left her front side and are moving in around her and passing her backside, while she still has her back to the goal. In this split second, you have the opportunity to receive the ball unguarded and send a shot to the goal. The key to cutting successfully, as always, is to keep one eye on the defender at all times. Know when she's watching you, and when she's zoned out watching the play or the ball.

A good body fake also helps with this cut. Pump your upper body and stick head in the opposite direction you plan on cutting. This causes her to start off on the wrong foot, which gives you an extra advantage. If, for example, you are facing her and plan on cutting around her toward your left, first step onto the ball of your right foot toward your right, move your stick head in that direction and pump your upper body to the right. Quickly recoil back by pushing off the ball of your right foot and pulling your stick head back in toward your body. Explode toward the left, moving quickly around her side and cutting sharply in behind her back. You're eliminating her from play, as well as moving yourself into a better offensive spot.

Front Cut

The front cut is similar to a slant pattern cut in football. Imagine the feeder is on the top of the restraining line. You are sprinting in toward goal down the right side of the field, coming up on a defender who is ready to take you on. When you reach the defender (for the purposes of this scenario, let's say that happens around the 12-meter area), stutter

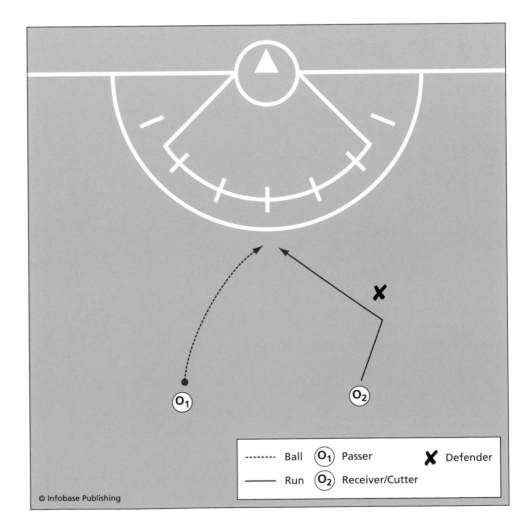

step in front of her to throw her off, and then cut in on a diagonal toward the goal. Your defender is on your backside away from where the ball is coming from. Essentially, you are boxing out your defender with your body. This cut eliminates her from the possibility of intercepting or interfering in any way with you receiving the ball. Show a target with your stick head as you cut hard, and receive the ball away from the defender. Pivot toward goal and slide a shot in around your defender, keeping her out of the play.

Scissor Cut

The scissor cut involves two players. The players start on opposite sides of the field and at the same time, they both cut on a diagonal toward the

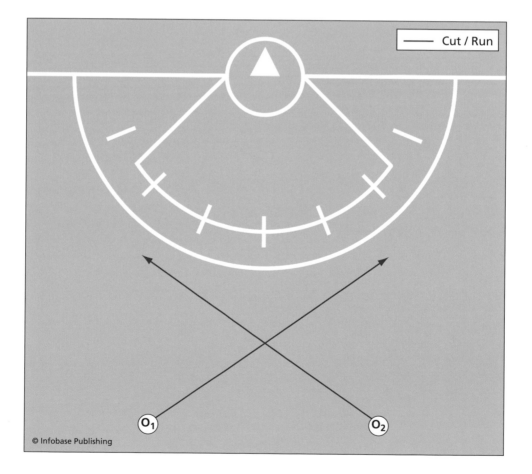

center of the field. They pass directly by each other at the center of the cut, and then continue moving on a diagonal so they end up swapping sides of the field with each other. The paths of the two players make an X on the field. This cut can be executed to simply move players around the field and create space.

The idea with this cut is to confuse the defense and get them to move. It's always more difficult for defenders to defend players who keep switching positions and sides of the field with each other. It makes the defense either have to run to keep up, or call out a switch with a teammate, which also leads to confusion on their end. Either way, you're making them work.

Pass and Cut

The simplest and most standard form of a cutting play is to pass and cut. It is one of the most fundamental playing styles of the game. The concept is relatively simple: every time you pass the ball, cut away from where you just passed. "Pass and move," says Coach Vesco. "Send the ball and move opposite of where you sent the ball." Cut hard, sharp, and with intention so your defender follows. With players passing and cutting, the field is in continuous motion and there is less chance for crowding. Coach Kiablick agrees, "Just like in basketball, start simple, and every time you pass, then cut." This is critical to learn as a beginner.

Give and Go

Another standard passing play is the give and go. Give and go is a quick series of passes between two players as they advance down the field. It is great to use to get around one defender in a two versus one situation. During the give and go, maintain a small passing distance to eliminate the possibility of interception and to keep the pace of the game moving.

Imagine player one has the ball as she approaches the defender. Player two is slightly ahead and to the right of player one. Once player one comes within one yard of the defender, she quickly passes the ball to player two. The defender follows the ball and steps toward player two.

Immediately after releasing the ball, player one cuts around the defender to the left, away from the side where player two is. Player one moves around the defender and cuts back in behind the defender's back toward player two. Player two, who has only briefly had the ball in her possession, sends a quick pass back to player one who is now beyond the threatening defender.

The two players continue to advance down the field side by side, passing the ball in a give and go formation against every defender they encounter.

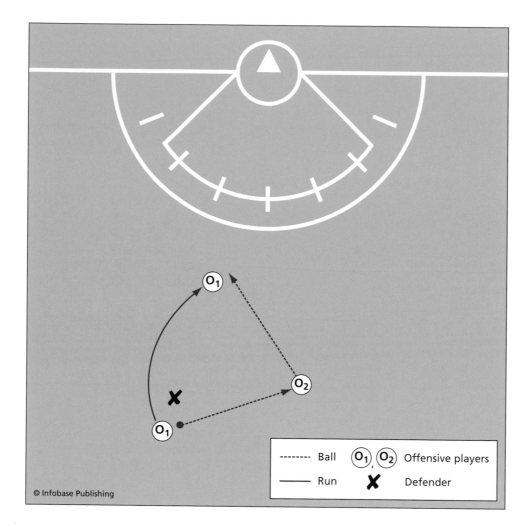

© Infobase Publishing

| -------- Ball | (O₁), (O₂) Offensive players |
| ———— Run | ✗ Defender |

THE PLACE TO BE

Four meters in front of the goal, within the eight-meter arc, is a four-meter square. In this spot, eighty percent of all goals are scored. As an attacking unit, this is where you want to shoot. If you are a feeder and you see an open teammate in this area, send the ball there immediately. If you have the ball and see this area open up, move in there immediately and shoot the ball.

SIMPLE OFFENSIVE CONCEPTS

There are any number of attack theories that can be developed in lacrosse. Patterns of attack are really just a series of cuts. When executing a play, only one or two cuts may result in a pass, while other cuts are decoys intended to fool the defenders. When you are cutting as part of a play you must always act with the same intensity as if you were about to receive the ball even if you know your cut is a decoy. You need your defender to think you're a critical part of the play and not let her leave your side.

Attack play in lacrosse is closely related to basketball style plays with sharp cuts, short passes and screening and picking. However, there is one difference: "The thing about lacrosse is that the more creative you are the better you can coach and play. In basketball there's set plays that everyone knows, but in lacrosse, coaches are always coming up with new plays," says Coach Kiablick.

Below are a few standard passing patterns used by coaches. However, as always in this sport, creativity is key. There is no right or wrong, so be creative in determining different plays.

Balanced Attack v. Unbalanced Attack

There are basically two styles of attack, a balanced style and an unbalanced style. As the name indicates, a balanced attack keeps the offensive team balanced across the field. "In general, you want to teach players to be balanced in attack. Not necessarily to play balanced, but to set up into a settled offense where they can work the ball around. Keeping it balanced is important because you want to have passing options," says Coach Kiablick.

Once your team crosses over into the offensive restraining line, if you are executing a balanced attack, then you have a setup where there are one or two players behind the goal, one player out on either side of the goal and two or three players across the top of the eight meter arc, alternately cutting in for a pass. In this style, when someone cuts to another place, the other players are constantly repositioning themselves to keep the field balanced.

In an unbalanced style attack, the number of attack players on one side of the field will far outweigh the number on the other side. "Side" in this context refers to the left, right, top of the eight-meter arc, or behind the goal. "Usually people run a balanced attack, but the unbalanced attack is where you're going to create the opportunities," says Coach Vesco. The strategy involved in this style of attack is that the side of the field where there are fewer players allows more space for dodging and scoring opportunities.

CALLING THE PLAYS: COMMUNICATION!

In order to get these plays off in an effective manner, someone's got to be calling them out. Often times a coach calls or signals for a certain play from the sidelines, however as your team matures and develops together, you may find that one offensive player—perhaps the one with the loudest voice—will call plays after getting word from the coach.

Teams use a variety of ways to signal for set plays. Words or numbers are the easiest to call; however, they are also the easiest for the defense to interpret. If "one" is called out three times in a row and the same thing happens each time, the defense will learn to break down the play before it even starts.

Some teams have color cards that they hold up where blue is one play and red is another. Some teams have the ball carrier give a sign to indicate the start of a play. If she holds her left hand up, her teammates know it's time for a certain set play. Whatever the style of communication, it's important that everyone is always paying attention and ready for it. "There are times," says Coach Vesco, "when people don't hear the plays and they'll be doing one thing when everyone else is doing another, and that's where the breakdown starts to happen."

Setting Picks

Setting a pick is a common term used in basketball, so if you have any basketball experience, this should sound familiar. Setting a pick is an off-ball offensive strategy. When you set a pick, you are positioning your body so it is more difficult for a defender to guard her attacker. You are not permitted to push or run into another player. You simply place your body in a critical space and stay there, forcing the defense to move around you.

Typical picking situations occur when the ball is moving into the 12-meter fan and eight-meter arc. As your team settles into its offense, you notice that one of your teammates is at the far right of the 12-meter fan with her defender facing her and positioned between her and the goal. You know that if that teammate moves around her defender, she'll be able to receive a pass from the ball carrier and get a shot off in front of the goal. You can help by setting a pick for your teammate.

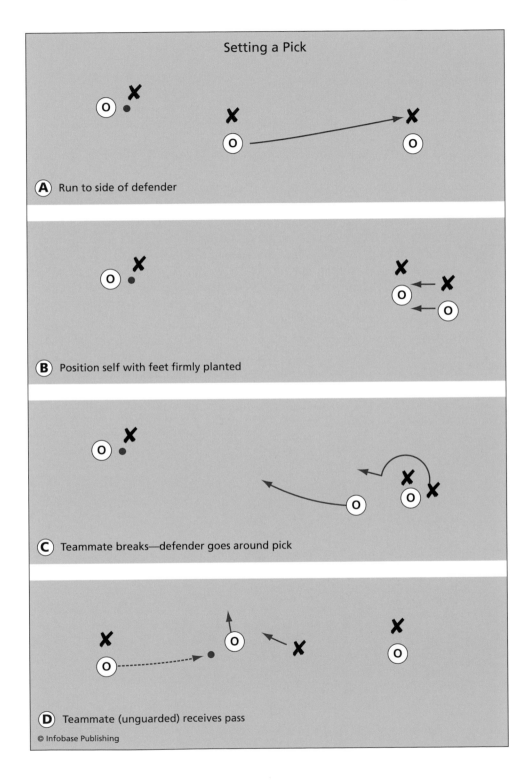

Setting a Pick

(A) Run to side of defender

(B) Position self with feet firmly planted

(C) Teammate breaks—defender goes around pick

(D) Teammate (unguarded) receives pass

© Infobase Publishing

Make eye contact with your teammate as you move in to set the pick. Run over to the defender and position yourself on her side, the side that your teammate intends to move toward when she cuts. Firmly plant your feet on the ground and stand facing the defender with your stick in front of you in a defensive stance. Your knees are bent and your weight is on the balls of your feet. You are stationary. Do not push into the defender and do not move your feet. You have just set a pick.

As soon as you get to this position, your teammate cuts hard around the defender to the side where you are positioned. The defender automatically attempts to follow her attacker. You, however, are blocking the defender's path so that she must move around you. When she moves, it is essential that you keep your feet planted on the ground. If you move your feet toward the defender, you will get called for a moving pick, or a pushing foul if you push her in any way. You have to be set in position before she changes her course and moves into you.

Timing is critical when it comes to setting a pick. It all happens very fast. If you give the defender too much time, she will figure out what you're up to and the pick will be wasted. You must be in communication with your attacking teammate to ensure that you both know what side to go to and when to go. This is primarily done with eye contact, however if you need to use verbal cues, call out "helping" to let her know you understand her need and are coming to help out. Avoid using terms as obvious as "pick" so the defense doesn't know exactly what is about to happen.

Stacking

Stacking is an example of an unbalanced attack. There are a variety of stacking options, including double stacks and triple stacks. The most basic stack is a single stack. Imagine the feeder has the ball behind the net. The coach calls a stacking play. All other attack players run to the set stack spot, which is typically at the top of the eight-meter arc, however it can also be more toward the left or right side, or even behind the goal if the feeder is at the top of eight-meter arc.

The stacking attack players line up one behind the other at the set point. Defenders follow the stacking attack players. This causes the defense to clump—a true disadvantage for them.

Once stacked, one-by-one (in order of who is closest to goal) the players run straight out of the stack toward the goal and cut alternating left and right. For example, the first player runs out and cuts hard to the left. The second player follows, starting her run as soon as the first player makes her cut. The second player then cuts hard to the right. Players continue running through until the stack is empty. At any time, the feeder passes the ball to a player who is open when she comes off the stack.

In a double or triple stack, the offense breaks into two or three lines around the eight-meter arc. In a double stack situation, three players are in each line. If executing a triple stack, two players are in each line. When the stacks go off, players cut out of the stack and can then do a variety of things: a player can cut out to receive a pass, or she can cut over to the other line to set a pick for a teammate. The more stacking and picking you have going on, the more confusing it is for the defense. Be creative with stacking, use it hand in hand with picking, and develop any number of offensive plays.

Decoy Stack

A decoy stack is set up exactly the same way as the stacking maneuver described above. In the decoy, you can use a single, double or triple stack. When the offense moves into stacking formation, the defense follows the players to their positions. However, the stack never goes off. The feeder dodges her defender, rolls the crease, and moves around to the front of the goal, sliding one in past the surprised goalkeeper.

Isolation Plays

An isolation play is when the ball carrier is isolated in a certain area within the offensive restraining line. All her teammates cut to another section of the field, bringing their defenders with them leaving the ball carrier with plenty of space to move around the field. During these plays, the ball carrier is usually the player with the best stick work and one-on-one capabilities. Isolation plays must be disguised—if the defense knows what's coming, they'll send a double team to the ball carrier to stop the play.

Flood

Another form of isolation play is called a flood. In a flood play, all players at the same time move to the right side of the field (or the left side, or the top of the 12 meter fan). That is, all but one player—the ball carrier. That player is then left alone on the empty side of the field with only her defender. This gives the ball carrier more room to move around her defender and get a shot off. She simply has to fake one way, explode past the defense in the other direction, and place the ball past the goalie—easy enough. The beauty of the flood is that there are no other defenders around to pop up and double team the ball carrier because they have all moved to the other side of the field. These types of plays have to be executed quickly, however, because eventually the defense will realize what is happening and will reposition to help defend against the ball carrier.

CENTER DRAW RULE CHANGE IN 2002

In fall 2002, a new rule went into effect regarding the center draw. Only five players from each team can be beyond the restraining line in the middle of the field and in play to receive the ball from the center draw. All other players (seven remaining on each team) must be within the restraining line to a goal. This new rule creates more space and frees up the players, allowing for more movement and less crowding during the center draw.

Center Draw

One of the most important offensive advantages of the game is winning the center draw. It is the first play of the game and it sets the tone for things to come. "All things being equal," says Coach Vesco, "if you're able to win the center draw consistently, you're going to win the game." The center draw is also used to resume play after a goal is scored.

The center draw is taken in the center circle in the middle of the field. Traditionally, as a center, you would face the direction you are attacking, however there has been a recent revolution in the center draws, and players now start with their backs to the goal they are attacking. This is called a left hand draw and it is very effective. Stand in the middle of the center circle with your back to the goal you are attacking. Your left hand is up on your stick about one to two inches from the stick head. Your right hand is on the butt end of the stick in the same position, as if you are holding a bike handle while you ride. Your knees are bent low and your weight is on the balls of your feet. This gives you a low center of gravity and more power. The ref places the two centers' sticks so they are back-to-back and parallel to the ground. The ref then puts the ball between the two sticks and balances it there. The two centers apply equal pressure to keep the ball balanced until the whistle blows and play begins.

When the whistle blows, it is your job to gain possession of the ball. This can be done through a variety of ways. Your first move is executed with your bottom right hand. "Rev" your hand forward so the stick pocket opens up and faces the sky. As you rev, turn your left wrist with the stick so your stick head is parallel to the ground. This causes the ball to drop into your pocket. Immediately pull up with your top left hand and send the ball hard over your head, so it is launched into your attacking end. Direct the launch to one of your attack wing teammates.

A second option is to pop the ball up and pass it to yourself. Again, rev with your right hand and turn your left wrist open. Then pull the ball up and slightly to your right, away from your opposing center. Use a short follow through when pulling up to pop the ball up high and out of your stick. If you use a long follow through, the ball will travel too far and you won't be able to get it. Once you've launched the ball up, extend your stick with only your right hand on the bottom of the stick and reach for the ball. Extending in this way gives you a greater reaching distance to gain possession.

A third option during the draw is to allow the opposing center to win the draw and let the ball go through to your defensive end. Do this when you know your defense is ready and is strong enough to get the ball and gain possession.

Whatever option you choose, the ball must travel outside of the 10-yard circle for the play to be legal.

> ### COACH KIABLICK'S CENTER DRAW TIPS:
>
> - To get a jump on the draw, don't just listen for the whistle, but watch the ref also. The referee starts with her arm up above her head, and drops her arm down as she blows the whistle to start play. If you have your eye on the ref, start with your first revving motion when she pulls her arm down. It's easier for your brain to process the sight of her moving her arm than the sound of the whistle.
> - If you're not winning the draw, jump up off the ground. "Get really low and actually come off your feet," says Coach Kiablick. This movement puts your body weight into your efforts and helps you to gain possession.

Fast Breaks

A team can suddenly go from being on defense to being on offense. This occurs when a goalie makes a save and keeps possession of the ball. Now the defenders must instantly look to move the ball down the field toward the opposing goal.

The goalie holds the key to an effective change of possession. She should yell "break," "clear," or something similar to alert her teammates that she has the ball, and they need to go on the offensive. The goalie can hold the ball for up to 10 seconds before she must pass it.

During this time, her teammates should spread out and look to get open. If the players remain close together, it's hard for the goalie to find someone to pass to. Defenders also can easily knock down or intercept a pass.

The goalie can look to the sidelines. It's usually safer to pass quickly to the side. Short passes down the middle can be intercepted more easily. More experienced goalies can try long passes down the field. Nothing gets a fast break off to a better start than a long, pinpoint pass. If a player catches the pass in full stride, she can almost immediately have a scoring opportunity by passing or shooting.

If you see a teammate preparing to catch a long pass from the goalie, don't just stand there and see if she'll catch it. Sprint down the field so you'll be ready to contribute. Your teammate may drop the pass or it may go over her head. Then you're in position to get the ball and keep it away from the defenders. Now you've kept the fast break alive. Once again, teamwork is critical.

DRILLS AND GAMES

Three Ball Star

Players: Five
Equipment: Ball and sticks
Distance: Five yards from each player

Form a five-prong star with five players. All players are five yards away from each other. One player starts with the ball and sends the ball two passes to her left. For example, player A is standing next to player B, who is next to player C, who is next to player D, who is next to player E, who is next to player A. Player A passes to player C, bypassing player B. Player C then passes to player E, who passes to player B, bypassing player A. This drill is teaching active thinking while playing. It is not just a game of catch; you must concentrate on whom you are passing to. Once the star is moving and everyone understands the game, add another level of play. After receiving the ball, fake a pass before sending the real pass two players away. Continue incorporating different functions, dodges, body fakes, stutter steps, or other footwork techniques, to make the game as lifelike as possible. Play for 10 minutes.

Give and Go

Players: Two
Equipment: 10 cones, sticks and ball
Distance: 100 yards

Using the entire length of the field set up one cone every 10 yards from goal line to goal line. Each cone is an imaginary defender. Start with the ball with your teammate slightly to your right, about five yards away. Run onto the "defender" with the ball and break down your steps as you approach. When you are one yard away from the cone, quickly pass the ball to your teammate who is to the right and slightly ahead of you. Once you pass, cut hard to the left around the "defender," then sharply cut back in behind the cone. Give a target with your stick and receive a pass back from your teammate. Continue this at every cone until you reach the end of the field. Switch roles so your teammate is now the ball carrier and you are supporting her. Do this up and back two times.

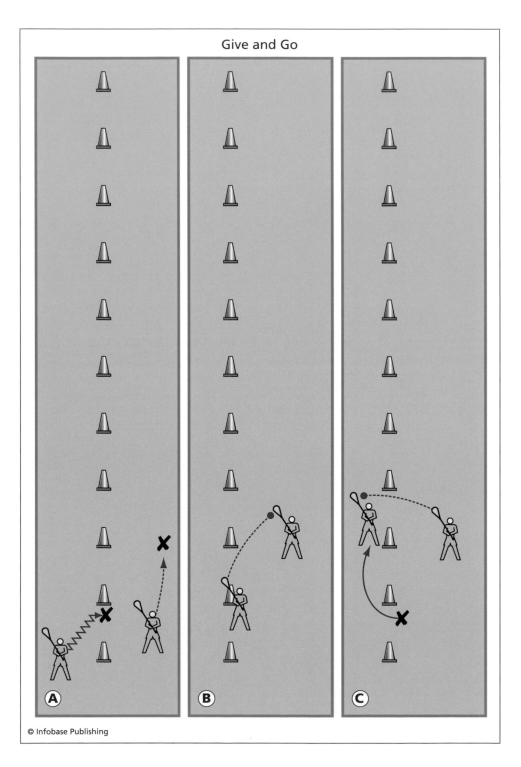

Give and Go

Four Passes

Players: Four plus goalie
Equipment: Four cones, sticks, ball, goal cage, and goalie equipment
Distance: Eight-meter arc

Create a four-meter square approximately four meters in front of the goal. Remember, this is the high scoring area. Place a cone at each corner of the square and one attack player at each cone. The goalie is in the goal.

One attack player starts with the ball and passes to a teammate, any one will do. The ball moves around the square in any order, however all four players must touch the ball. When the fourth player receives the ball, all attack players yell "SHOT!" The fourth player to receive the ball immediately turns to goal and shoots from her cone. The goalie blocks the shot and clears it out to one of the players and the game begins again. Keep track of how many goals are scored and how many shots are blocked.

Front Cut Feed

Players: Three
Equipment: Sticks, pile of balls
Distance: Restraining line

In this drill, two players are on attack and one player is a defender. The defender is not actively pursuing the ball, but is there to let attackers understand where defenders will be. One attack player stands next to the pile of balls on top of the 12-meter fan. The second attack player starts at the restraining line on the right side of the field. The defender is at the 12-meter area, in front of the second attack.

The second attack sprints in directly toward the defender. When she comes within one yard of the defender, she stutter steps, fakes to the right, and cuts hard in to the left, heading toward the goal on a diagonal. The defense moves with her, staying behind her. The defender's stick is up, but she is not actively pursuing the ball. Once the second attack makes this diagonal cut and has the defender on her back side, she gives a target with her stick head, making sure to keep the stick head in front of and away from the defender. Player one passes the ball to the target. Player two receives the ball, pivots toward goal and shoots.

Feed, Shoot, and Run

Players: Six
Equipment: Pile of balls, sticks
Distance: Up to restraining line

Divide the group in half. One group forms a line to the right of and behind the goal. The second group forms a line to the left of the goal at the eight-meter arc. The first group is the feeders, and they have the pile of balls next to them. The second group is the shooters. The first person from the second group cuts in to goal showing a target. The first person in the first group feeds the ball. The shooter receives the pass and immediately shoots. Once the shot is off, the feeder sprints to the midfield line and then jogs back to the end of the shooting line. The shooter sprints around the back of the goal to the end of the feeder line. Continue this drill for 15 minutes.

As you progress in this drill, add another line at the top of the eight-meter arc. One player from each line cuts in to goal showing a target, and the feeder must decide whom to pass to. This introduces the feeder to the decision-making aspect of her role.

Three v. Two on the Move

Players: Five
Equipment: Sticks and balls
Distance: Restraining line to goal

Three offensive players start at the restraining line, one in the middle, one on the right side of the field and one on the left side. Any one of the players starts with the ball. Two defenders start at the goal line on either side of the net. The offensive players begin moving in to goal, and the defenders sprint out. One defender pressures the ball; the other stays back to offer cover protection.

The attack is focusing on cutting and passing through the defense. No attack player can hold onto the ball for more than 15 seconds: receive, pass, and immediately cut away from where you passed the ball. Focus on eye contact, body language, and stick head targets.

Two-Minute Drill

Players: At least six plus goalie
Equipment: Pile of balls, sticks, goalie equipment, and three cones
Distance: Restraining line to goal

Set up three cones at the restraining line. The first cone is slightly to the left of the center of the field, the second cone is slightly to the right of the center of the field, and the third cone is farther to the right of the field. One player stands behind each cone. A pile of balls is behind the goal.

Player one at the first cone has the ball. Player two (at the second cone) cuts hard away from the player one for one yard, then pivots, and switches back cutting hard toward player one. Player three sprints straight ahead toward the goal line. When player two begins cutting back, player one passes her the ball. Player one then sprints directly toward the goal.

Player two receives the pass and pivots towards goal. Player two sends a long pass down to player three, who completed her sprint to the goal line and cuts back to receive the pass.

Player one, who began sprinting in toward the goal, is just reaching the top of the eight-meter arc when player three receives the long pass. Player one calls for the ball at the top of the eight, and player three feeds her the ball. Player one then shoots the ball on goal. Player three cuts around the back of the goal, running back up to the restraining line on the side where the first cone is. Player two sprints behind the cage, picks up a ball from the pile and passes to player three. Player three passes to the next person at the first cone, and the drill begins again.

This is a fast moving drill. Start out slow and understand what each role is expected to do, and then put it to a sprint. Do this continuously for two minutes.

Maze Craze

Players: Seven
Equipment: Sticks, ball
Distance: 20 meters

Six defenders set up in a two-one and two-one format, so there are two upside-down triangles next to each other with all players facing the same direction. The two defenders at the top of the triangle are four meters from each other, with one defender between them and four meters back. The next two defenders are four meters behind the one defender, and four meters away from each other. The last defender is behind the second set of two defenders and is four meters behind them. All defenders are in the defensive position with two hands on their sticks.

You are the attack player. You have the ball in your crosse. Your goal is to move through the defenders—first moving between the two and then around the one, then between the next two and finally around the final defender—without getting checked. The defenders can check if they have a clean check when you are in their area, however they cannot chase you. As the attacker, move at top speed through the maze. Duck around oncoming checks, protect your crosse, and accelerate to move through the defense.

One v. One with a Feed

Players: Seven plus goalie
Equipment: Goalie equipment, goal cage, sticks, and balls
Distance: 12-meter fan

One attacker and one defender are in the center of the eight-meter arc. The goalie is in the cage. Four feeders stand in a square around the 12-meter fan, two across the top and two across the bottom. Each feeder has two balls. One defender is behind the goal "on call." The attack player in the eight-meter makes a cut to receive the ball from any one of the four feeders. When she is free—and only when she is free—the feeder sends her the ball. As soon as the attack player receives the ball, the second "on call" defender comes out from behind the cage to double-team the attack player. The attacker, meanwhile, receives the ball and immediately turns to shoot. She does not want to hold onto the ball for long since she knows the double is coming.

Continue through until each feeder has sent the ball into the attacker. There is no set order, but the attacker is not through in the center until she receives the ball from every feeder.

9

Team Defense

THE BASICS

There is nothing more satisfying than shutting down a strong offensive unit. So far, you have learned how to guard one-on-one against an attack player. You know how to hold your stick in the proper position in order to keep the attack player out. You can move with your opponent because you have quick footwork. But when there is an entire offensive unit moving toward you, you need to work with your defensive players to form a force to counter that attacking unit.

The defensive unit is a team in itself, a working subunit of the 12 players on the field. When the ball crosses over the defensive restraining line, defenders work together to stop the ball, eliminate passing options, and transition the ball to offense. The key to doing all this successfully is to communicate and talk with each other in direct, supportive language.

The ultimate objective in defense is to prevent a score. But there are other aims too. For instance, good defenders can break up or intercept passes. They can hustle after and recover loose balls. They can disrupt the rhythm of the attacking team. They can force ball carriers away from the center of the field, to the sidelines, where passing and shooting accurately become more difficult.

Good defense involves the proper attitude. You must be aggressive. Don't stand around and watch as the opposing team moves down the field. Challenge the ball carriers. As the offense gets closer to your goal, you must move closer to the ball carrier.

Keep your stick high, instead of letting it drop down to your waist. Slide your hands low on the stick so you'll have greater reach and can more effectively break up shots or disrupt the ball carrier.

As you guard the ball carrier, stay aware of what's happening on the rest of the field. Take note of where her teammates are and where she may be passing the ball next. Maintain a proper stance and posture so you can effectively move up or back, left or right, to stay with your opponent.

Keep your feet shoulder width. Lower your butt and keep your back straight. Keep your weight balanced. Don't be too rigid or too relaxed. If a ball carrier gets past you, don't give up on the play. Hustle and catch up, then get back into position in front of her to disrupt her movement.

Most of all, never turn your back to an offensive player. That gives her a green light to streak past you and make an accurate pass or take a shot on goal.

Communication

Communication is the foundation for solid team defense. "It's so important to have great communication on defense. Even if you're not the fastest in the world, you can be a great unit together with great communication," says Coach Vesco. Your entire team, especially the defensive unit, must all work together and know where all the opposing attack players are and who are the most dangerous. It is virtually impossible for one person to be able to see, assess, and process all that information.

"You have to be able to know when there's a fast break coming, when to step up on ball, when to hold back, or when go to the double team," says Coach Vesco. There's a lot going on in the backfield, and it's practically impossible to handle it all yourself. Don't forget, in this game players are running behind the goal—you'd literally have to have eyes in the back of your head to see everything. So rely on your teammates and trust that they are going to let you know everything they see. Similarly, get your vocal chords going. Talk to your teammates to let them know that you are there to help them. A large part of successful communication isn't just directing traffic, but supporting players when they do well, too.

Always use direct, supportive language when communicating with your teammates. Coach Kiablick suggests setting certain words for specific situations. "Call 'with you' to let your teammate know you're with her and she can force her player into you for help. Call 'pick' when you see a pick, or 'switch' when you see a switch," she says.

Coach Vesco also points out that most of the defensive communication is lead by the goalie. From the back of the field, the goalkeeper has the best view of the playing field. No matter what, it's critical that as a defender, you always listen to your goalie first. "Most of the communication is done by the goalie. She can see the whole field and see what's happening," says Coach Vesco.

THE ENTIRE DEFENSIVE UNIT

The entire defensive unit consists of not only the defensive field players, but also includes the goalie. All players—not just the goalie—must understand that they are all working together to stop a goal from being scored. "The defensive unit and goalie need to understand that they are both part of the defensive unit. The goalie is not her own entity, and neither is the defense," says Coach Wescott.

Too often, players—and even coaches—break these two forces apart. In order for the team to operate as one, these forces must unite. And it's not only the players' responsibility to do that. "[As a coach,] you create the unity of a defensive unit and a goalie, it doesn't just happen. So you have to teach them how they help each other and how to communicate with each other, and you need to teach them *all* to take the brunt of a goal," says Coach Wescott.

Positions

One simple way to divide defensive roles on the field is to breakdown responsibilities by positions. Although some positions require more defense than others, every player on the field must be prepared to be a defender at any time. Even if you're an attack player, it's essential that you know how the defensive unit works. There are times when you will be needed on defense. In order to be the best all-around player you can be, you must understand how the whole team works and be a part of that team.

An integral part of good defense is understanding how far your goalie comes out of the crease during defensive plays. This is the goalie's individual preference. Some goalies may prefer never to leave the crease, while some may constantly be shooting out to go for the ball. Either way, this affects the way the defense plays the game.

Goalie

The primary job of the goalkeeper is, in fact, to stop the ball from going into the net. The goalie blocks shots, clears to teammates, and often times chases loose balls outside the cage. However, she is also part of the defensive unit. Although a separate chapter focuses on the specific duties of the goaltender, she should not be considered a separate entity.

Point

The point is the most defensive field player. The point and the goalie work hand in hand to give voice to the defense as a unit. They are the eyes and ears of the backfield. Point is the last line of defense before the goalie. She always marks her opponent player-to-player. This means that as a point, you are right in your opponent's face and you stay with her wherever she goes in the defensive area.

UNITING THE DEFENSE

It is critical that the entire defensive unit bonds, especially the goalie and the defensive field player leader. This field player leader is either the point or the coverpoint. "The backbone of your deep defense and the goalie must bond," says Coach Wescott. The coach can ensure that the two form a strong relationship too. "Make them do things together. Make the defender warm up the goalie everyday. You need to get those two to bond," she says.

Coach Wescott also points out that it's best to pair a goalie and defender who are near the same age. "You don't want a senior with a freshman goalie. You want people who are going to be together for a long time, at least a couple years," she advises.

Coverpoint

The coverpoint is an integral part of a strong defense. On certain teams, the coverpoint (rather than the point) works with the goalie as the defensive leader. When the ball transitions quickly to defense, it is the coverpoint who is the decision maker in the backfield, yelling for others to get back and help out. The coverpoint usually marks the second home. If necessary, coverpoint also picks up any unmarked opponent in front of the goal.

Third Man

Third man marks the third home. In defensive situations, the third man picks up any unmarked opponent shooting through into the attacking area. The third man is quick and has great reflexes. She often intercepts passes and transitions the ball back to offense.

Defensive Wings

The defensive wings mark the opposing team's attack wings. When the ball comes down one side of the field, the wing on the opposite side of play moves deeper down the field toward the defensive goal. In this role, you offer cover support to your teammates. Defensive wings must be in excellent shape, as the position requires constant running up and down the field in transition from defense to offense.

Center

Center has many jobs. She is the most athletic player on the field and is required to do a number of tasks. A center is responsible for, in order of priority, marking, connecting with both offense and defense, assisting the defense, and transferring onto attack. When the offense moves over the defensive's restraining line, the center must get back there to help out and mark up. Center usually marks the opposing team's center, however she should get back and pick up the most dangerous player who is not marked. The center is a connection between offense and defense, and is required to do a lot of both.

Attack Wings

At any time, any one of the attack wings may be back on defense. Seven attack players and seven defenders are allowed within the restraining line at any time, so when all seven offensive players cross over, as a defender you know you need seven of your teammates helping out. If the center doesn't make it back for some reason, an attack wing is called upon to help. Although the point or coverpoint may call out for this help, as an attack wing you must be aware of this responsibility and initiate the help on your own.

DEFENSIVE POSITIONING: THE TRIANGLE

As a defender, you must always be positioned between the ball, the attack player, and the goal you are defending. Consider these three points to make up the three corners of a triangle. Within this triangle, always position your body so you are ball side/goal side. Always keep your attack player in front of you and square your shoulders to that player. Now slide slightly so you are one step closer to the ball than your attacker (ball side). When the ball crosses over the defensive restraining line, move closer to your opponent and keep her within one stick length.

Within this triangle, your rear end points toward the goal so you are closer to the goal than your attack player (goal side). If you see your goalie making a save, you are out of position. You must always be between your mark and the goal on defense. In this position, you are always forcing the attacker toward the outside of the field.

"It's a game of inches in every sense of the word, and you want to force the attack wide, and force them away from the goal cage. If you make them shoot two steps farther away from the cage, that could be everything," says Coach Wescott. You are the obstacle that prevents the attacker from moving straight onto goal.

Whenever a defender is on the ball carrier, she is in a pressure role. All other roles—those marking players one, two, or three passes away from the ball carrier—are in cover roles. The job of the cover roles is twofold. First, cover defenders eliminate the players they are marking as passing options by tightly marking them. Secondly, cover defenders are available to help out the pressure role on a double team.

Pressure

Whenever you are marking a player with the ball, you are in a pressure role. In this role, focus on the marking skills discussed in Chapter 4, and think about the triangle. You always want to keep your player toward the outside of the field. Your shoulders are square to the attack player, and your body is defensively positioned so she is forced to travel away from, never toward, the goal. Swivel your hips so your feet always move in the same direction as your opponent.

AGGRESSIVE PRESSURE

When there are enough cover roles supporting the pressure role, the pressure defender has the freedom to really step up onto the attack player. An aggressive pressure player moves right up onto the ball carrier and really gets in her face. Coach Kiablick discusses one very aggressive pressuring style in which the defender holds her stick with both hands stacked in fists around the butt end of the stick. Hold your arms straight out in front of you, extending them directly toward the attack player. Your bottom hand is in a fist around the butt end of the stick, and your top hand is in a fist around the stick, directly on top of the bottom hand. The stick head faces the opponent, but is angled back toward your own face, so your fists and the butt end of the stick are closest to the attacker. Your knees are bent, your weight is on the balls of your feet, and your eyes are on the ball. Approach the attack player, staying within your triangle and forcing her to the outside of the field. Move right up to the attack player and keep your arms straight out. This approach will immediately intimidate the attack player as you move into her space. Although this is an aggressive style play, it is perfectly legal since you are not pushing the attack player. Do not bend your arms and do not come in contact with the attack, but simply move close into her space. When she takes a step back to gain space, take a step forward and stay with her. This aggressive style play is sure to fluster her and cause her to lose the ball.

The aggressive-defensive style approach is slightly reliant on the ball carrier making a mistake. If you are right there in her face, you're taking the gamble—which is usually a successful one—that she is going to panic and lose the ball or make a bad pass. However, there is the chance that she will make a move around you. If this happens, you need to know someone in the cover role will step up and pressure the ball again. That is why this approach is best used when there are many supporting cover roles behind the pressure player.

Pressuring Behind the Cage

Imagine the attack team is settled around the 12-meter fan and the feeder is behind the cage with the ball. Typically, this is the start of an offensive movement, and as defenders you must be ready for anything. Everyone is marking and waiting. While the ball is behind the cage, there is no scoring threat. Whether or not to pressure the ball behind the cage in this situation comes down to coaches' preferences. Some coaches prefer to let the ball carrier stay back there and keep the defense on the front end of the cage, where the high danger is. As long as the ball is in back of the goal, no one is scoring.

However, other coaches teach to pressure behind the goal. "Some teams will play pressuring ball behind the cage and the defenders need to fluff enough to realize they're vulnerable around the crease when they do that," says coach Wescott. In other words, if defenders are behind the goal pressuring the ball, it leaves the offense more room in front of the goal—in the scoring area—if the feeder gets a pass off. Other defenders still in front of the goal must be aware of these scoring threats.

Coaches usually opt to pressure behind the cage if the feeder is incredibly patient and the ball stays back there for a long time. It may be necessary to move toward her and pressure the ball in order to make something happen. According to Coach Wescott, pressuring the ball behind the cage is dependent on the defenders involved in the situation. "It depends on how quick the defenders are and what they can handle. The more we go out to pressure the ball and pressure covers, the better we have to be communicating because we may get beat and need help," she says.

Off-Ball Positioning

Off-ball positioning refers to the cover roles mentioned above. Whereas the pressure role is the defender marking the ball carrier, cover roles are those who are marking players one or more passes away from the ball. In other words, it means that you are anywhere but directly on the ball carrier.

A general rule of thumb for off-ball positioning is to drop back if the ball is on the opposite side of the field from you. If you are on the left side and the ball is on the right, drop back on a diagonal from the ball and cheat in toward goal. You are always moving within the triangle discussed above, however your angles change as the ball moves around. If the ball comes over to your side, step up to either pressure ball or pressure players close to the ball. Your teammates on the other side of the field drop back on a diagonal away from the ball and move closer in to goal. By moving with this diagonal mentality, you create a solid line of supportive defense. If the ball happens to move through one side of the field, defenders from the other side are back and ready to step up and pressure the ball.

Marking Adjacent Players

You are marking an adjacent player if your player is next to the ball carrier and is one pass away from her. In this situation, the best defensive move is to continue to mark tightly, eliminating your player as a passing option. If a pass is attempted, you are close enough to go for the interception.

In this tight marking position, keep your body relaxed with your knees bent and your weight forward on the balls of your feet. Your feet are slightly wider than shoulder width apart. A wider stance helps you react more quickly to an interception. It also gives you a wider view of the field. Be prepared with your drop step and shuffle steps so you always keep your attack player in front of you, with your body between her and the goal cage.

THE HIGH SCORING AREA

"Eighty percent of the goals are scored inside the eight-meter marks within four meters of the goal cage," says Coach Wescott. It stands to reason, then, that as a defender you want to keep the attack players out of that area. No excuses!

The area is a four-meter square in the eight-meter arc, approximately four meters from the goal cage. Mark it off and know this area well. Together, your defensive unit needs to mark players out of the area, double team when necessary, and do whatever is called upon to prevent the attack from moving into that high scoring area. Often times, coaches mark this area with tape, spray-paint it a different color, or even pour baby powder on it during practices to get the defense aware of exactly where it is. "That's our home," says Coach Wescott, "and we don't let anyone come in and steal the house."

Two or More Passes Away

As a beginner, focus on staying with your mark whenever you are within the defensive restraining line. However, as you become more advanced in your play, a common defensive strategy is to move a step or two off players who are two or more passes away from the ball carrier and who are not a scoring threat. When you step off, cheat in toward the eight-meter arc. By moving in toward the eight-meter arc, you are making yourself available to help out other teammates who are in more dangerous situations.

For example, if you are two or more passes away, you can slide over to help a teammate with a double team if needed. "When you get to a higher level of play, you might not want to mark an off-ball player as tightly because the player with the ball is the one that's the concern, so be there to help with a double team," says Coach Kiablick.

Double Team

Occasionally you or your defensive teammate is faced with an opponent who has exceptional stick work and who is moving to the goal. As a defensive unit, the entire team has to work together to recognize that this is a potential problem. When this happens, one defender moves over to work with the marking defender to double team the attacking opponent. If you are marking a player who is two or more passes away, as described above, you are in the best position to slide over and help your teammate with a double team because your player is not dangerous at the moment.

Slide means you quickly move over to your teammate and the ball carrier. When you slide, always call out to your teammate that you are coming over to help. Defensively, your teammate is positioned more toward one side of the attacker—the goal side. You move into the area on the other side of the ball carrier, so that the attacker now has a defender in front of her on either side. Keep the ball carrier between you and your partnering defender. Maintain a distance of one stick length, and never move more than one step ahead of the ball carrier. Together, you and your teammate channel the ball carrier away from the goal.

While on either side of her, you and your teammate must divide responsibilities. One defender focuses on the stick, and the other focuses on the body. If you are on the stick side of the attack player, call out "stick," and slightly pressure her stick. Keep your stick mirroring the attackers stick. Do not make a move to stick check. Your teammate, similarly, calls out "body" to indicate that she is focusing on the ball carrier's body. In both positions, your feet are moving in the same direction as the attack player. If you are on the body side, you are paying attention to directing her body. Hold your stick in the barrier position, as you did when executing a body check.

In a double team situation, do not execute a stick check unless you are 100 percent sure that you will get the ball. By continuing to pressure her and direct her out of a dangerous area, you are taking her out of the game. In most cases, the ball carrier does something to lose control of the ball. "A lot of times if you're doing a good double team (especially in the eight meter), you want to hold back on a stick check because the attack ends up checking themselves by running into your stick," says Coach Kiablick.

In this situation you want to keep two hands on your stick. However, Coach Kiablick suggests that if the ball carrier attempts to cut out of the double team, meaning that she makes a move to pull out and cut around you, take one hand off your stick and "make yourself big." Remove the hand closest to the direction the attacker is attempting to cut and hold that arm out to the side, palm facing the attack. Your presence in that space deters her from moving in that direction. "Just taking your hand off your stick and extending it the way [your opponent wants to go] gives the offensive player the perception that it's not an open lane," says Coach Kiablick.

Defending Against Picks

As mentioned in the chapter on offensive strategy, a common offensive move is to set a pick for a cutting teammate. In the pick-setting scenario, an attacker moves onto one of her offensive teammate's defenders. She approaches and stands to one side of her teammate's defender. As she comes to this position, the offensive teammate cuts around the defender, moving to the side where her attacking teammate stands. The defender cannot simply follow her "mark" because the offensive teammate is in her way. This is a pick. It's great for the offense, but not so fun for the defense.

The first step in defending against a pick is to recognize when one is being set and step around it. If you are paying attention, the offense won't even get an extra step on you with their attempted pick. If it's too late and you run into the pick, call a switch with a teammate. Your teammate who was guarding the player who set a pick takes your cutting attacker, and you stay on the picking player.

In addition, if you see a pick in action, call out "pick" to make sure everyone knows what is going on. You can't defend against it if you don't know what it is. Constant communication is, as always, the cornerstone of successful defense.

ONE STICK LENGTH AWAY!

When you are marking within the eight-meter arc, remember that you must be within one stick length of your opponent. If you're more than one stick length away, it is a three-second violation or a shooting space foul. A three-second violation means you have been farther than one stick length from your opponent for more than three seconds. A shooting space foul means that you are directly in line to the goal cage but not marking anyone—you are in a shooting space. In this space you are in danger of getting hit with a shot.

Recovery

At times, the opposing team will forge its way down the field into your defensive end. This could happen in a fast break style, or it could just be that the offense has an extra step on the defense. Whenever this happens, the defense must get back, and get back quick. In the defensive world, this is called recovery.

When you recover back, make a beeline for the goal. Wherever you are on the field, move in a straight sprint back to goal holding your stick with one hand and keeping your body in the center of the field. As you recover back, note where the ball is and be sure to keep the ball carrier toward the outside of the field. Outrun the ball and gain defensive positioning, and then come up on her and pressure her toward the outside of the field.

Another recovery scenario occurs when one of your teammates is back alone on defense when the other team begins its offensive push. Your teammate needs help! She'll call for you to recover, and you sprint back toward goal. If your teammate is moving onto ball, continue recovering behind her and then pick up the next most dangerous player. If the ball is moving into the eight-meter area, this is the player closest to goal.

Player-to-Player v. Zone

There are two basic defensive styles that teams use: player-to-player and zone. The most common of the two is player-to-player in which each defender marks one attack player. The defender stays with that attack player and moves EVERYWHERE the attacker goes. The only time this changes is if the attack sets a pick and defense has to call a switch. Player-to-player is the foundation of team defense: Every player needs to know how to play it.

> ## REMINDER
>
> If a ball is loose and heading out of bounds, you get possession if you get to it first. The closest part of the player to the ball—including her stick—is what counts here. So stretch out your stick using a one handed grip to reach the out of bounds spot to gain the advantage and gain possession. Even if you can't get to the ball first, you must run as fast as you can to get in a good defensive position to stop the attack player from having a clear path to the goal. Remember, once the ref blows the whistle, everyone freezes until play starts again. If you slack off in your out of bounds chase, your opponent will start with the ball and possibly an unobstructed path to the goal.

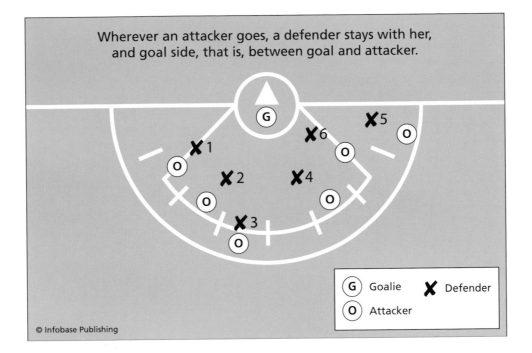

A zone defense is based on the same premise in the sense that you are marking a player. The difference is that you don't stay with one particular player the entire time. In zone, each defender is responsible for a certain defensive area in the 12-meter and eight meter areas. As a defender, you mark whoever comes into your area. "I think you have to be a great man-to-man communicating defense to play a good zone, because zone is man-to-man, it's just the people in your area," says Coach Wescott.

The trouble with this is that sometimes more than one attack player comes into your space, which means that one of your teammates has no one in her space. That teammate must slide over to help you out. Zone defense requires everyone to always be paying extra attention to everything happening within the defensive restraining line. It takes a lot of concentration and skill. "It's hard to play a good zone," says Coach Wescott.

Zones are sometimes used for short periods to disrupt an offense. They can also be used when your team is down a player because of a penalty. In a zone defense, players are responsible for an area, not a particular player, so it's possible to compensate for having fewer teammates.

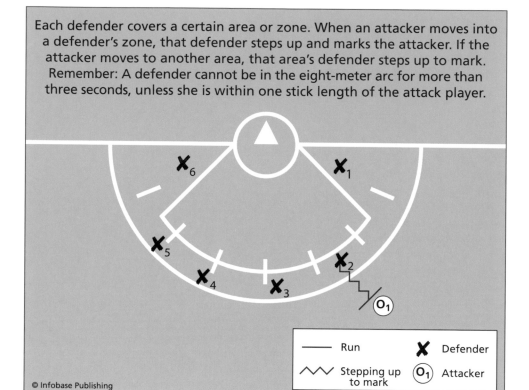

Each defender covers a certain area or zone. When an attacker moves into a defender's zone, that defender steps up and marks the attacker. If the attacker moves to another area, that area's defender steps up to mark. Remember: A defender cannot be in the eight-meter arc for more than three seconds, unless she is within one stick length of the attack player.

—— Run	✗ Defender
⋀⋁⋀ Stepping up to mark	O_1 Attacker

© Infobase Publishing

Zone defense in eight-meter arc and 12-meter fan

Zone defense takes more discipline to play. Players must avoid their natural instinct to follow their opponent wherever she goes. Instead, the defensive player must stay within her designated area and cover whoever comes there.

Teams that have outstanding defenders probably shouldn't use a zone defense very long. Aggressive defenders who can anticipate plays need to be free to follow their opponent and create a turnover—not simply stay at home and wait for a defender to enter their zone.

Good offensive teams can beat a zone more easily than good man-to-man coverage. A zone defense, naturally, leaves more open spaces on the field for the offense to maneuver. But try to use both zone and man-to-man coverage during a game. The more you can do to keep the offense off balance, the better chance you have to prevent goals and create turnovers.

DRILLS AND GAMES

Setting Angles

Players: Five plus goalie
Equipment: Sticks, ball, goalie equipment
Distance: Eight-meter arc

Two offensive players and two defensive players set up within the eight-meter arc. One offense is on either side of the arc, and the defenders are marking them. The goalie is in the crease.

The feeder is outside the eight-meter arc and has the ball in her stick. She is not going to pass, and no shots are taken during this drill. The feeder moves around the top of the arc and the offense and defense in the eight-meter arc adjust their positions when she moves. As the feeder moves, the attack players pull out or cut into a spot where they can receive the ball. The defenders move with them, staying within the defensive triangle and keeping their rear ends pointing to goal and their bodies facing the attackers. Defense also thinks about positioning so they can intercept if a pass is thrown. The goalie is also moving around the cage, practicing her angles.

Start this drill off slowly, with the feeder slowly moving around the top of the arc. The idea is to make sure defenders understand where to be positioned as the ball comes over the restraining line. Speed up the movement as this concept is learned. Eventually, have the feeder pass the ball into the attack players. Defenders should go for the interception if they can, but otherwise focus on their body positioning to keep the attack from moving onto goal.

Four Passes

Players: Eight
Equipment: Four cones, sticks, and ball
Distance: Eight-meter arc

Set up four cones in a square at the top of the eight-meter arc. The cones are four meters from each other, outlining the high scoring area discussed earlier. One attack player stands at each cone. One attack starts with the ball. In the center of the square is one defender. The other three defenders are waiting behind the goal. The attack players pass the ball around the square, in any order, however all four must each receive the ball once. Once all four have received the ball, the player with the ball takes a shot.

It is up to the one defender in the square to stop the shot from being taken by intercepting the ball during the four passes. When that defender intercepts the ball, a second defender comes in and joins her in the square. The offense starts over with four passes, and together the two defenders work to intercept the passes. If the defense intercepts again, a third defender comes out to join them and the attackers start all over again. Continue until there are four attackers and four defenders.

If the attack gets a shot off and it goes in the cage, they get one point. If the defense gets an interception, they receive one point. Keep score of the game. Once the game reaches four on four, play in a game-like setting until the attack scores or the defense gains possession and gets the ball out of the restraining area.

Three v. Two Continuous

Players: 11 plus two goalies
Equipment: Two goals, eight cones, sticks, balls, goalie equipment
Distance: Full field

In each restraining area on each end of the field, set up one goalie in the cage and two defenders. At each restraining line, set up two cones four meters from each other on the far right of the field near the sideline and two cones four meters from each other on the far left of the field near the sideline. The cones are all on the restraining line. Inside each set of cones stands one player. These players are the outlet passes. On one end of the field, in front of the defenders, stand three attack players in the left, middle, and right side of the field.

All together, there are two goalies (one in each net), four defenders (two with each goalie), three attack players (inside the starting end 12-meter fan) and four individual outlet players (one in each set of cones on the restraining line). Play starts at the end of the field with three attack players.

The goalie clears the ball out to one of the attack players. The three attack then move onto goal. The two defenders must work together with the goalie to stop ball and gain possession. When defense comes up with the ball, they send it out wide to one of the outlet players. That player then becomes the ball carrier and moves offensively down to the other end of the field.

The two players who were just on defense convert with the one ball carrier and sprint down to the other end of the field. These three are now the attack players. The end of the field they are heading to has two defenders and a goalie waiting for them. The same three-versus-two situation happens now at the other end of the field. The defense passes the ball to one of the outlets when they come up with it, then the three new attackers head down to offense.

Meanwhile, the players left behind when the defense converted to offense switch roles. The outlet player who wasn't used moves to a defense role with one of the attack players. The other two attackers stand in the cones on either side of the field to be the outlet passes. This is a continuous drill and it is very fast moving. Continue this drill for 15 minutes.

Three Blind Mice

Players: Six plus goalie
Equipment: Three blindfolds, sticks, balls, goalie equipment
Distance: Restraining line

Blindfold two defenders and the goalie. Station the defenders in the 12-meter fan and the goalie in the cage. One defender starts at the top of the eight-meter arc and is not blindfolded. Two offensive players start with the ball outside of the restraining line. The third attack player is the ball carrier and is behind the cage and far to the right side of the field. When the coach blows the whistle, the offense begins moving down the field and the ball carrier begins moving, too. The defender without a blindfold tells her defense where to go in order of importance, so she starts first with the goalie. The defender's commands must be concise and clear. She says the goalie's name, and then says exactly what she wants her to know, "Mary, the ball is behind the goal line out to the right." Once the command is complete and Mary knows what's going on, she takes off the blindfold and plays the ball. The defender then moves on to the other defenders, directing them to the other players moving down the field. The defender without the blindfold must move to the ball carrier as she calls out commands so that the offense doesn't gain an advantage. This drill gets the defenders talking and trusting each other.

Four v. Three with Recovery

Players: Seven plus goalie
Equipment: Sticks, balls, goalie equipment, one cone
Distance: 40 meters

Three defenders start in the eight-meter arc. The goalie has the ball. Four attack players are on the restraining line spread across the field. One cone is 10 meters beyond the restraining line toward the center of the field, roughly 40 meters from the goal line. This cone is to the left or right side of the field.

The goalie clears the ball out to one of the attack players. Once the goalie releases the ball, one defender sprints up to the cone, circles it, and recovers back. As she is sprinting, the offense has a four on two advantage. The offense quickly works the ball down the field to take advantage of this defensive shortage. Once the defender recovers back, she calls to her teammates to let them know she's back, and then picks up the most dangerous player not marked.

Player Ride

Players: Five plus goalie
Equipment: Sticks, balls, goalie equipment
Distance: 50 yards

The goalie starts in the goal with the ball. There are two attack players—one on each far corner of the 12-meter fan along the goal line. Three defenders are across the field, one on the far right side of the field about five meters from the goal line, one in the center of the eight-meter arc five meters from the goal line, and the third on the far left of the field about five meters from the goal line.

The goalie clears the ball to one of the two attack players. As soon as the attack receives the ball, she begins moving down the field. The goal of the attack is to get the ball over the 50-yard line. Once the attack receives the ball, defense moves onto her and immediately double teams her. The attack teammate moves over to help her attack partner, trying to cut away from the defender marking her.

If the defense gets the ball away from the attack, the three defenders shift to offensive roles and bring the ball to goal, attempting to score. The two attack players shift to defense and it becomes a three-versus-two situation, with goalie.

Knockout

Players: Seven
Equipment: Sticks, balls, four cones
Distance: 25-yard by 25-yard grid

Place four cones in each corner of a 25-yard square. Inside the cone are three attack players who each have a ball, and four defenders. Each of the attack players starts along a different side of the square. The four defenders are in the middle of the square. The attack players must move the ball around the grid, each working into a space, not into each other.

The goal of the defense is to corner an attack player by working with each other to double team or force attackers into each other. Defenders check the attack players to gain possession, and then send the ball out of the grid. Once an attacker's ball is sent out of the grid, she is done the game and must leave the square. If the defense forces an attacker out of the square, the attacker is done. The game is complete when the defense forces or gains possession and no attackers are left in the grid.

Give the attack players a time limit of 45 seconds. If all three survive the defense for that time period, the attack wins.

10
Conditioning

LACROSSE IS A GAME OF NONSTOP ACTION FOR 50 MINUTES—60 MINUTES at the collegiate level. You need to keep your body in the best physical condition possible to ensure that you are playing at top level through the entire game—and the entire season. You must train for endurance so you can survive the length of the game and for speed so you can keep up with your opponent and outrun her. You must strengthen your muscles so that you are a strong competitor. Proper conditioning can separate good players from great ones. Lacrosse players serious about succeeding must be aware of conditioning year round. That doesn't mean you train fanatically at all times. Instead, it means you don't totally neglect training during the off-season, then desperately try to get in shape as the season approaches.

Conditioning has many benefits. It can reduce the possibility of injury and speed recovery time if you do get hurt. It can improve your agility and balance—key qualities in the fast-paced, free-flowing sport of lacrosse. You must be able to start and stop quickly, as well as move fluidly forward and backward and left and right.

In this chapter, we'll also discuss nutrition. In recent years, coaches and trainers have put increased emphasis on what athletes eat and drink. In general, avoid sugary and highly processed foods. Eat plenty of fruits, vegetables, whole grains, and dairy products.

Some players (or their parents) hire private trainers to craft individualized nutrition and training plans. This may or may not be necessary. Your school or team may have coaches and trainers who can give excellent advice on nutrition and training. Also, there are many online resources.

No matter what sources you consult, get serious about conditioning. You'll see almost immediate results in how you feel and play.

178

GETTING STARTED: STRETCHING

Before starting any kind of activity, first warm up and stretch out. Slowly jog two laps around the perimeter of the field to start warming up your muscles. Once your muscles are warm, it's time to stretch them out. Stretching is essential to developing flexibility and preventing injury.

When stretching, stretch your muscles to the point of tension. Once you reach that point, hold the stretch for 20 seconds. If your muscle begins to shake, relax the stretch slightly—you've gone just beyond the point of tension. The tension lessens as you hold the stretch, and by the time 20 seconds is up, your muscle is loose and relaxed.

Do not overstretch (hold a stretch for too long) or overextend (reach too far) on a stretch. If you are in pain when you stretch, stop the stretching action. Stretching is intended to prevent pain, not cause it.

Create a routine and work through that routine everyday. Start with your neck and shoulders, and then move down through your upper arms, wrists, and hands. Focus on your back, torso, and hips. Then move onto your legs—your quads and hamstrings, as well as your calves and ankles. By developing a routine, you're preventing the risk of missing a muscle group when you stretch, which results in injury.

While you are stretching, always take deep breaths in through your nose and out through your mouth. When you breathe as you stretch, you send a fresh supply of oxygen to the muscle being stretched. This keeps that muscle healthy and happy and in prime condition. Do not worry about how far you can stretch. Don't think that because your teammate can touch her nose to her knee, you should, too. If you continue with a steady stretching routine, eventually you will notice an increase in your flexibility.

Stretching also relaxes your body and mind and helps you focus on the upcoming workout or game. A well-planned stretching routine makes you sharper mentally and physically.

Neck

Drop your head to the right side so your right ear is facing down toward your right shoulder. Continue dropping your head until you reach the point of tension, then hold for 20 seconds. Relax your shoulders as you do this stretch. Bring your head back to the upright position, and then drop your head to your left so your left ear is down to your left shoulder. Hold at the point of tension for 20 seconds.

Bring your head to the upright position. Keep your shoulders relaxed and your body facing forward. Turn your head and look back over your right shoulder as far as you can. Hold this position for 20 seconds. Relax

Neck rotation

and turn your head to look over your left shoulder. Hold again for 20 seconds.

Repeat these stretches twice.

Shoulders

Stand up straight with good posture. At the same time, lift both shoulders up towards your ears and rotate backward in small circles. Complete 10 backward circles. Stop and change direction, rotating your shoulders forward in small circles. Complete 10 front circles.

Shoulder shrug

Extend your right arm straight out in front of you and pull it across your chest. With your left hand, hold your straight right arm across your breast. Hold for 20 seconds. Switch arms.

Triceps

Extend your right arm straight up over your head so your elbow touches the side of your head. Bring your left hand to your right elbow, and bend your right arm at the elbow so your right hand drops behind your back. With your left

Triceps stretch

hand, pull your right elbow behind your head until you reach the point of tension. Hold for 20 seconds. Switch arms and repeat.

Wrists

Stand straight with good posture. Hold your arms out at the side of your body. Keeping your arms straight, rotate your wrists in small circles towards the back of your body. Complete 10 small circles, then switch and rotate your wrists in 10 frontward circles. Repeat twice.

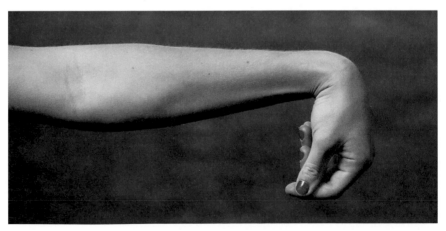

Wrist stretch

Side stretch

Side Stretch

Stand upright with your legs slightly wider than shoulder width apart. During this exercise, it is important to keep your upper body in line with your lower body. With your knees straight and your hips stationary, bend at your waist toward your right side. Drop your right arm down to your knee, and reach with your left arm over your head toward the right. Remember to keep your body in the same plane as you do this stretch. Keep your rear-end tucked in and do not lean forward. When you reach the point of tension, hold for 20 seconds.

Switch sides and stretch to the left, bringing your right arm over your head and reaching toward the left. Hold for 20 seconds.

This exercise is great for stretching the sides of your torso, which is so important in lacrosse. Maintaining a flexible trunk helps you when you are dodging, cradling, and shooting on goal. The more movement you have in your upper body, the better you'll be able to control the ball and confuse your opponent.

Hips and Butt

Sit on the ground with your legs extended straight in front of you. Bend your left leg at the knee and cross your left foot over your right thigh, planting your foot squarely on the ground. Wrap your arms around your left knee and hug your knee, pulling it closer to your chest. Feel this stretch in the left gluteus maximus muscle and your hip. Hold for 20 seconds.

Hip stretch

Return your leg to the extended position, and then switch legs and hold for 20 seconds.

Hip Flexor

The hip flexor extends from the top of your thigh to your trunk. This muscle allows you to walk and run, so take good care of it. From an upright

Hip flexor

position, drop down into a sprinter's crouch with your right foot forward. Your entire right foot is on the ground and your right knee does not extend beyond the toes of your right foot. If it does, bring your foot forward until your toes reach beyond your knee. Place your hands on the ground on either side of your right foot.

Extend your left leg out behind you, so only the ball of your left foot is on the ground. Push the top of your left leg down toward the ground, bending your knee slightly. As you do this, you will feel a stretch in your hip flexor. Continue to the point of tension and hold for 20 seconds.

Relax and switch legs.

Groin

Sit on the ground with your legs extended out in front of you. Touch the soles of your feet to each other, and bend your knees, pulling your feet in toward your body. Keep your knees as close to the ground as possible. Once you reach the tension point, stop pulling and hold for 20 seconds.

If you are more flexible in the groin and you don't feel tension when you bring your feet in toward your body, lean your chest over your feet to stretch the muscle. Hold for 20 seconds.

Groin stretch

V Stretch

Sit down on the ground and extend both legs out to either side in a V with your toes pointing up to the sky. Lean forward with your chest, reaching your arms straight out in front of your shoulders. You will feel this stretch in your back and in your groin and inner thighs. Hold for 20 seconds, and then pull your upper body back to the sitting position.

Next, lean over your right leg with your chest. As you lean down, twist your torso and lead with your chest, keeping your shoulders centered over your right leg. Extend your arms straight out, reaching toward your right toe. Hold for 20 seconds, return to the starting position and switch sides.

V stretch

Seated Stretch—Hamstrings

Sit down on the ground with both legs extended in front of you side by side. Place your hands on each thigh and slowly walk your hands down your legs toward your feet. Bend at your waist as you move closer to your feet. Keep your knees straight and remember to breathe.

Continue stretching down toward your feet until you reach the point of tension. If you are very flexible and you can reach your toes easily, pull them back toward your body to get the full effects of this stretch. This

Seated stretch—hamstrings

stretch works on your hamstrings, as well as your back. Hold for 20 seconds and relax.

Hamstring

To isolate the hamstring, lie on your back with your legs stretched out straight. Pull your right leg up to your chest and hold your leg behind your knee. Pull your right leg toward your chest until you reach the point of tension. Keep your left leg extended straight out and completely touching the ground. Hold for 20 seconds. Slowly return your right leg to the ground. Switch legs and repeat.

Quads

It is critical that you really work to stretch out your quadriceps muscles, the large leg muscle on the front side of your thigh. This large muscle can cause an unbelievable amount of pain if damaged, and takes a long time to heal.

Stand upright with good posture and shoulders back. Slowly bend your right knee and bring your right foot up behind your body to your rear end. Grab hold of your right foot with your right hand. Maintain your balance and hold for 20 seconds. You will feel your quad stretching

Quad stretch

out. If you have a hard time keeping your balance, focus on one spot on the ground. Keep your eye on that spot and do not look away.

Release your right foot, returning it to the ground, and switch sides.

Calves

Stretching your calves and Achilles tendon is also essential. Every time you push off your foot in a sprint, you are using those muscles. Stand with your feet next to each other and bend at the waist until your hands touch the ground. Walk your hands forward until your heels lift off the ground. Relax your left heel, allowing it to come up off the ground and keep your right heel touching the ground. You will feel this stretch in your right calf. Hold for 20 seconds.

Now bend your right knee and keep your right foot on the ground. You will feel the stretch move down your leg to your Achilles tendon, just behind your ankle. Hold this for 20 seconds. Walk your hands back slightly and switch legs. Repeat.

Ankles

Stand upright with your feet shoulder width apart. Raise your left leg so only the ball of your foot is on the ground. Rotate your left ankle, moving your heel in small circles to work the ankle out. Complete 10 circles and relax. Switch legs and repeat.

Calves stretch

EXERCISES FOR INJURY-FREE KNEES

These exercises will help prevent rupturing the anterior cruciate ligament, or ACL, of the knee. More than 60 NCAA Division 1 soccer programs have tested these exercises and reduced knee injuries by more than 70 percent among their athletes. The exercises focus on balance, core stability, hip control, knee alignment and stability, cutting or change of direction while running, jogging, and running.

HOPPING SIDE TO SIDE

Starting position. Hands on hips, legs slightly bent at knee, feet shoulder-width apart. *Movement.* Hop or jump a short distance, two or three feet, laterally to the left. Maintain control of your weight on landing and keep the upper leg, or quadriceps, aligned straight (facing front, the leg forms a 90-degree angle to flat surface) over the knee. Hop or jump to the left, or back to starting position. Five repetitions, two sets.

HOPPING, UP AND DOWN

Starting position. Hands on hips, legs slightly bent at knees, feet shoulder-width apart. *Movement.* Jump straight up and land in same position, keeping upper leg aligned straight over knee. Ten repetitions, two sets.

BALANCING ON ONE LEG AND BALL TOSS

Starting position. Stand with feet shoulder-width apart, holding ball in one hand. *Movement.* Lift and fold one leg backward at knee, balancing on one leg. Toss ball up and catch. Pass ball around your back. Switch legs and repeat. Five reps, two sets.

ONE-LEG HALF KNEE-BENDS (WITH PARTNER)

Starting position. Two players stand alongside each other, shoulder to shoulder, each placing her closest arm on the other's shoulder. *Movement.* One player bends outside leg at knee and stands on other leg (closest to partner or teammate). Player slowly lowers herself without losing balance and keeps bent leg from touching the ground. Partner or teammate helps maintain balance of one-legged teammate by allowing her to grasp shoulder. Partner repeats exercise. Partners switch sides and exercise opposite legs. Five reps, two sets.

TOE RAISES

Starting position. Hands on hips, legs and body in half knee-bend position, that is, legs bent at knees, spine at 45-degree angle, and upper legs parallel to ground. Slowly straighten legs and rise onto toes, head and spine in alignment. Ten reps, two sets.

BODY RAISE AND HOLD

Starting position. Lie on stomach, back straight, head facing forward, feet and legs pressed together, arms bent at elbow with lower arms flat (or parallel) on surface. *Movement.* Slowly raise body—contracting core muscles in stomach and back—onto toes, spine straight. Hold for 30 seconds, five reps.

TORSO LIFT

Starting position. Lie on left side, left arm bent at elbow and in front of body angled 90 degrees from spine; bend left leg at knee and tuck behind and under the body angled at 90 degrees (with spine). Straighten right leg with inside of right foot touching surface. *Movement.* Lift torso up forming straight line from toes to head. Hold for 30 seconds, five reps.

RUNNING THE CONES

Note: Each of the running exercises requires two rows of five cones set side by side or laterally approximately seven yards apart at intervals of approximately 10 yards each.

Starting position. Stand behind cone number one. *Movement.* Jog around the cones five times. Five reps, one set.

RUN THE CONES, SHUTTLE BACK

Starting position. Stand behind cone number one. *Movement.* Jog to the second cone, stop and run backward, stopping at the second cone. Repeat the forward running (two cones) and backward running (one cone) till you reach the fifth cone. Two reps, three sets.

RUN THE CONES, SIDE HOPS

Starting position. Stand behind cone number one. *Movement.* Run to the next or second cone, stop, and hop sideways to the opposite cone, circling it and returning to cone number two. (You will hop or shuffle in one direction going to the cone and in the other direct when returning.) Run forward to the next cone and repeat movement at each cone. Two reps, three sets.

RUNNING

Lacrosse is a game of constant movement and speed. To be the best player you can be, you need to develop a running workout and stick to it. Incorporate both long runs as well as sprints into your workout.

The running world can be divided into two groups: speed and endurance. For some people a 100-meter sprint is a walk in the park. For others, an eight-mile run is more appealing. You need to determine what kind of runner you are, and then you need to work twice as hard to develop the less appealing trait.

Some people believe, erroneously, that speed can't be improved—that you're either born fast or you're not. But with today's advanced training methods, players can increase their speed significantly. We'll discuss some specific exercises later.

GOOD FORM

Before starting any running workout, make sure you are in good running form. Proper body positioning during a run makes the workout more enjoyable. Always maintain excellent posture when you are running—that means shoulders back and chest forward. Keep your shoulders dropped and relaxed so your neck feels very long. Your triceps are next to your ribs and your elbow is bent so your forearm and upper arm form a 90-degree angle, with your forearm extending straight out in front of you.

As you run, drive your elbow on the same side as the foot moving forward straight back. Make sure you are always pumping your arms in this way when you run; it helps to maintain your good posture and solid breathing. It also sustains your momentum.

Down below, your toes are always pointing in the direction you are running. Don't let your toes drift out and point away from your body, and don't run pigeon-toed with your toes pointing into each other. Always explode off the balls of your feet, lift your knees high and land your stride on the balls of your feet. Running on your heels gives you a flat-footed form and makes your run more awkward.

Finally, maintain even breaths as you go. Always breathe in through your nose and out through your mouth.

Endurance

To get into optimal shape for the season, you should run an average of three to five miles about three or four times a week. As your skills advance and you progress as a player, it becomes incredibly important for you to focus on your body conditioning and endurance. Starting three months in advance, tie on your favorite running sneakers and hit the road or the trail. If long runs don't appeal to you, work your way into them.

Break down your first week of exercise to ease into the running spirit. On the first day, run one mile. On day two, run two miles. Take the third day off, and on day four, run two miles. Day five run one mile and day six go to the track to work on sprints (see below). Rest on the seventh day.

On week two, step it up a notch. Start the first day with a one and a half-mile run, and the second day with a two-mile run. Rest the third day and on day four go out for a one and a half mile run. Come back on day five with a two-mile run. Hit the track on day six.

On week three, run three miles the first day, one the second, and rest on the third. Come back on the fourth day with one and a half miles, and take it back up to three on the fifth.

As you increase your endurance from week to week, up your mileage. Never increase more than 20 percent of your distance from one week to the next. Slowly increasing your mileage prevents injury. If you start exercising three months prior to the start of the season, you'll be in top form for the first practice.

You can also break up your runs with days of lifting weights in between (more on lifting weights comes later in the chapter). Once you're up to three miles throughout the week, alternate running and lifting days, and give yourself two days off per week. During the season, your coach will develop a training program for you and your team.

RUNNER'S WORLD

Always drink plenty of fluids when you run. If you're going out for longer than one hour, bring a bottle of water with you for the road. Sip the water, don't gulp it down, to avoid cramping. Avoid drinking ice-cold water—it can be a shock to your system. If you're working in a hot climate, run early in the morning or in the evening after the peak heat hours. Proper hydration improves your performance and endurance and reduces the chance of muscle cramps. If you don't drink enough while training or playing, you can suffer dehydration or heat exhaustion. Listen to your body. Bring plenty of fluids to practice and games. Get in the habit of taking breaks to drink water or a sport drink.

Sprints

The other important aspect of running is sprints. You need to be as fast as you can possibly be, and most of this comes from practice. "You have to be in great shape to play this game," says Coach Verso. "You don't necessarily have to go out and run 10 miles, but work on a lot of stop and go sprints."

Make sure you warm up and cool down after every sprint workout. Two laps around the field at a slow jog is good for both getting your muscles ready for a workout, as well as settling them down after you're done sprinting. And don't stop for too long between sprints. Your muscles are more likely to cramp up if you're stopping and starting through the workout.

Five Yards Alternating

One easy way to work on your training is to head over to the lacrosse field. Jog two laps to warm up, and then stretch out thoroughly. Start on the goal line and run the length of the field, alternating between sprinting and jogging every five yards. When you get to the other end of the field, rest for one minute. Then run back the length of the field, alternating sprinting and jogging every five yards again.

Zigzag Sprints

Another good workout you can do to increase your sprinting ability is to start on one corner of the field where the goal line and sideline meet. Jog straight up the sideline to the restraining line, then pivot and sprint across the field on the restraining line. When you reach the opposite sideline, turn toward the 50-yard line and jog along the sideline to the 50. When you reach the 50, pivot and sprint across the field along the 50-yard line until you reach the opposite sideline. Slow to a jog again and run along the sideline to the far restraining line. Sprint across the field along the restraining line, then jog to the goal line. Pivot and sprint along the goal line until you reach the sideline. Jog back the length of the field to the spot where you started.

Falling Starts

Another excellent way to strengthen your sprints is to do what is called a falling start. In a falling start, you use your body weight to get your momentum going forward. Stand on the end line with your feet next to

Falling start

each other. Stand on the balls of your feet and lean forward until it feels like you're about to fall on your face. At the last possible second, step forward and catch yourself, "falling" into a sprint. Sprint through to the restraining line. When you reach the restraining line, rest. Fall again and sprint back to the goal line. A falling start works on your first foot explosion, so when you take off in a sprint during a game, your first step will be powerful and sure to beat your opponents.

SPEED DRILLS

There are other ways that you can enhance your speed skills in addition to sprints. These are slightly more creative than sprints. Have fun with these, but remember to fulfill each movement so you don't shortchange yourself during your workout.

High Knees

Maintaining excellent posture, run forward lifting your knees through to at least waist level. With each step you take, drive your knee straight

up and through your waist. Pump your arms to really get your knees up high. This is not a race. The important part of this exercise is to get your knees up high, not to accelerate forward or be the first to finish. Lift your knees in this way for 50 meters. You will feel your quads burning as you do this exercise—that means it's working.

Butt Kicks

Keeping your good posture, run the next 50 meters kicking your rear-end as you go. Overexaggerate the flexion of your knee as you go and drive your foot all the way through to your rear-end. Again, this is not a speed race to the finish line. The goal is to focus on this

High knees

Butt kick   High knee skip

particular motion, which isolates your hamstrings and will ultimately strengthen your sprint.

High Knee Skips

Skip for 50 meters driving your knees high through your waist. Step forward to start your skip and bring your first leg high up through your waist. Pump your same side arm down as you drive this knee up. Continue through, bringing your knees higher each time. Feel the workout in your calf and Achilles tendon, as well as your quads.

Grapevine

Extend your arms straight out to your sides to balance yourself. Stand sideways and step laterally with your right foot, extending your foot beyond your shoulders. Bring your left foot in, crossing it in front of your right

Grapevine

foot. Step out again with your right foot, and then pull your left foot in, crossing it behind your right foot. Continue moving laterally, alternating the left foot in front of and behind your right foot for 50 meters. Always stay on the balls of your feet when doing this exercise.

Figure 4

Figure 4

This improves flexibility and strength of the leg and hip muscles. Standing with legs shoulder-width apart, lift and fold one leg as if squatting on floor. Grasp leg at the ankle or foot. Pause and raise body up off heel and onto toes. Repeat with other leg. Begin with five repetitions and increase to 15, adding two more reps each day.

Fire Hydrant

This exercise improves balance and lower body strength, especially the hip flexor muscle. Stand with feet shoulder-width apart, raise knee of one leg to waist, and pass foot and leg over an imaginary fire hydrant, rotating the leg a full 90 degrees before lowering to ground. Repeat with other leg. Begin with five repetitions and increase to 10, adding one more rep each day.

Fire hydrant

Lateral Cone Jump

Place one cone on the ground and stand next to it. Keep your feet together and jump sideways over the cone. Land on the balls of your feet and immediately spring up and return over the cone to your starting position. Jump laterally over the cone for 30 seconds.

STRENGTH TRAINING

Another important piece of the puzzle is to strengthen the muscles that you use in the sport. The main muscles to focus on are your arms and upper body since most of the work is done with the crosse, however you also want to strengthen your stomach and torso to gain strength and flexibility.

Push-ups

There's nothing better than good, old-fashioned push-ups. Lie on the ground on your stomach and move into a push-up position with your legs straight and the balls of your feet on the ground. Your hands are on the ground, palms down, and fingers pointing forward. Your hands are slightly wider than shoulder-width apart. Keep your body straight, do not sag at your waist and bend your back. Your hips may have a tendency to drop toward the ground—this is poor form. Keep everything in a straight line in your body. Bend at your elbows and bring your chest toward the ground. Your head is up and your eyes are looking forward. Continue down until your elbows reach a 90-degree angle. Then push your body back up to the starting position. Complete 15 push-ups.

If you are having a hard time with the push-up, bend your knees until they touch the ground. Keep your knees on the ground and your body in a straight line. Do the push-ups with your knees on the ground.

Push-up

Crunches

Lie on your back with your legs bent at the knees. Cross your ankles and lift your feet up off the ground so your hips are at a 90-degree angle to the ground. Place your hands next to each ear with your elbows pointing out to the sides, keeping your shoulders on the ground. Lead with your chest and lift your upper body off the ground, touching your left elbow to your right knee. Keep your knees stationary and bring the elbow to the knee, twisting your torso as you go. Come back down to the ground and crunch up again, bringing your right elbow to your left knee.

Crunch

Do not place your hands behind your head and pull your head up. This exercise works your stomach muscles. Repeat this for 20 crunches.

Leg Lifts

Another excellent form of exercise is leg lifts. Sit on the ground with your legs extended straight out in front of you. Start with your right leg. Point your toe and lift your leg off the ground at a 45-degree angle. Keep your knee straight and your toe pointed. Hold your leg in this position for two complete seconds, and then lower to the ground. Once the back of your leg touches the ground, bring your leg up again to the same position. Complete 15 leg lifts with your right leg. Relax your leg and switch to your left leg. Repeat.

This exercise strengthens your quad and hip flexors. It is simple and can be done anywhere, and it's very effective.

Weight Lifting

Weight training is often misunderstood. Some players think weightlifting makes you stiffer and less flexible. In fact, the opposite is true.

Weightlifting, done properly, improves flexibility, as well as strength. And don't worry about becoming bulked up. Unless you use supplements that can be dangerous (and illegal), you won't develop large, constricting muscles.

Weight training is really a subject for an entire book. In short, exercises exist that target specific areas, such as chest, shoulders, arms, and legs. If you've never lifted weights, consult someone who has. He or she can teach you about repetitions, sets, and rest during a weightlifting session.

Safety is an important consideration in weight training. Some exercises require a spotter, or someone who stands beside you in case you try to lift too much. The spotter helps you safely put up the weight.

NUTRITION

The final component of working out is eating right. Always try to maintain a balance between carbohydrates, proteins, and fat. Eat an even amount of meat, dairy products, and fruit and vegetables to maintain a solid supply of energy to get you through your workouts. As your exercise habits increase, so will your appetite—this is completely natural. Remember to drink a lot of water as you increase your activity too. Soda and other carbonated drinks will dehydrate you and can cause cramping and fatigue.

ASSOCIATIONS AND WEB SITES

The following associations and Web sites are a sampling of many great lacrosse organizations. To find more or those in your area, start here or search the Internet.

Intercollegiate Women's Lacrosse Coaches Association (IWLCA)
http://www.eteamz.com/IntercollegiateWomensLacr/

IWLCA national contacts:

Gothard Lane
Executive Director
Telephone: (443) 951-9611
E-mail: glane.iwlea@comcast.net

Ricky Fried
Division I Representative
Telephone: (202) 687-2420
E-mail: pgfzz@georgetown.edu

Cecil Pilson
Division II Representative
Telephone: (814) 824-3066
E-mail: cpilson@mercyhurst.edu

Mary Ann Meltzer
At-Large Representative
Telephone: (313) 578-0415
E-mail: meltzer@ncaa.org

Melissa Falen
NCAA Committee Chair—Division III
College of Notre Dame
4701 North Charles Street
Baltimore, MD 21210-2404
Telephone: (410) 532-3585

Fax: (410) 532-5796
E-mail: mfalen@ndm.edu

Kristen Selvage
President
Telephone: (570) 893-2414
E-mail: kgeissle@lhup.edu

International Federation of Women's Lacrosse Associations (IFWLA)
http://www.womenslacrosse.org

IFWLA contacts:

Fiona Clark, President
51B Southern Cross Circle
Ocean Reef
Western Australia 6027
Australia
E-mail: fiona2@iinet.net.au

Sue Redfern, Vice President, Administration
14 Osborne Road
Kingston
Surrey KT2 5HB
England
E-mail: sue.clegg-is@btinternet.com

Jackie Hufnell, Vice President, Rules and Umpiring
64 Sundance Drive
Elverson, PA 19520
E-mail: jmhuffs@aol.com

Jenny Haynes, Vice President, Competition
Hawthorns
99 High Street
Iver, Bucks SL0 9PN
England
E-mail: jennyhaynes@hotmail.co.uk

Denis Wescott, Vice President, Education and Training
101 Irishtown Road
Emmitsburg, MD 21727

LaxLinks: Lacrosse's Launch Pad
http://www.laxlinks.com

National Collegiate Athletics Association (NCAA)
http://www.ncaasports.com/sports/w-lacros/ncaa-w-lacros-body.html

NCAA Membership Services
P.O. Box 6222
Indianapolis, IN 46206-6222
Telephone: (317) 917-6222
Fax: (317) 917-6622

US Lacrosse, Inc.
http://www.lacrosse.org
113 West University Parkway
Baltimore, MD 21210-3300
Telephone: (410) 235-6882
Fax: (410) 366-6735
E-mail: info@uslacrosse.org

Youth Lacrosse USA: The Source for Youth, College and
    Professional Lacrosse Information
http://www.youthlacrosseusa.com

FURTHER READING

Adams, Jen. "One-Hand Wonder." *Inside Lacrosse.* (November 12, 2002): 64.

American Sports Education Program. *Coaching Youth Lacrosse.* Champaign, Ill.: Human Kinetics, 2003.

Brackenridge, Celia. *Women's Lacrosse.* Hauppauge, N.Y.: Barrons Educational Series, 1978.

Delano, Anne Lee. *Lacrosse for Girls and Women.* Dubuque, Iowa: WMC Brown Company Publishers, 1970.

Fisher, Donald M. *Lacrosse: A History of the Game.* Baltimore, Md.: Johns Hopkins University Press, 2002.

Grauer, Neil A., and David G. Pietramala. *Lacrosse: Technique and Tradition.* Baltimore: Johns Hopkins University Press, 2006.

Hanlon, Thomas W. *The Sports Rules Book: Essential Rules for 54 Sports.* Champaign, Ill.: Human Kinetics Publishers, 1997.

Hanna, Mike, and Jackie Pitts. *Lacrosse for Men and Women.* New York: Hawthorn/Dutton, 1980.

Hoyt-Goldsmith, Diane. *Lacrosse: The National Game of the Iroquois.* New York: Holiday House, 1998.

Howarth, Kath, and Bobbie Trafford. *Women's Lacrosse: The Skills of the Game.* Wiltshire, U.K.: Crowood Press, 1989.

Kurtz, Agnes B. *Women's Lacrosse for Coaches and Players.* Hanover, N.H.: ABK Publications, 1979.

Morris, Daniel. *Confident Coach's Guide to Teaching Lacrosse.* Guilford, Conn.: Lyons Press, 2005.

National Alliance for Youth Sports. *Coaching Lacrosse for Dummies.* Indianapolis, Ind.: Wiley Publishing, 2008.

Perez-Mazzola, Vincent, *Lacrosse Training Bible*, New York: Hatherleigh Press, 2007.

Price, Robert G. *Ultimate Guide to Weight Training for Lacrosse.* Pepper Pike, Ohio: Price World Enterprises, 2005.

Samaras, Crista. "Center Stage." *Inside Lacrosse* (November 12, 2002): 58.

Stanwick, Sheehan. "Rock and Roll." *Inside Lacrosse* (November 12, 2002): 62.

Tucker, Janine. *Baffled Parents' Guide to Coaching Girls' Lacrosse.* Camden, Maine: Ragged Mountain Press/McGraw-Hill, 2003.

INDEX